G. Lamprecht

Introduction to
FORTRAN 77

G. Lamprecht
Introduction to SIMULA 67

W. Werum and H. Windauer
Introduction to PEARL

Günther Lamprecht

Introduction to
FORTRAN 77

Friedr. Vieweg & Sohn   Braunschweig / Wiesbaden

CIP-Kurztitelaufnahme der Deutschen Bibliothek

Lamprecht Günther:
Introduction to FORTRAN 77 / Günther Lamprecht. –
Braunschweig; Wiesbaden: Vieweg, 1986.
ISBN-13: 978-3-528-03360-6   e-ISBN-13: 978-3-322-89421-2
DOI: 10.1007/978-3-322-89421-2

1986

Produced by Lengericher Handelsdruckerei, Lengerich

Preface

Fortran is one of the most common programming languages in the field of science and Fortran compilers are available for almost all computers and are being increasingly used by personal computers.

The initial standard version of Fortran IV has been extended enormously due to the large range of computers available and the numerous requirements demanded of them. As a result of this there are at present a vast number of Fortran "language dialects" which impairs the exchange of programs. Fortran 77 is a new language standard which includes many of the previous extensions. Furthermore, Fortran 77 subset has been developed which takes into consideration the limited possibilities of small computers.

This book is intended, by means of examples, to introduce the reader to the programming language Fortran 77, whereby the liminations of Fortran 77 subset will be taken into consideration. The examples and exercises have been chosen so that the solutions can be arrived at with a minimum of specialized knowledge. The reader will thus, with the exception of a few statements, be able to become acquainted with all possibilities of Fortran 77.

I would like to take this opportunity to thank G. Parker for his translation of this book from German into English, Dr. S. Bartnitzke for critical reading of the manuscript and Mrs. U. Kleinschmidt for typing the text.

Bremen, February 1986   Günther Lamprecht

Contents

Introduction

The following illustration shows the different stages that
have to be processed from the initial formulation of a problem
up to its final solution:

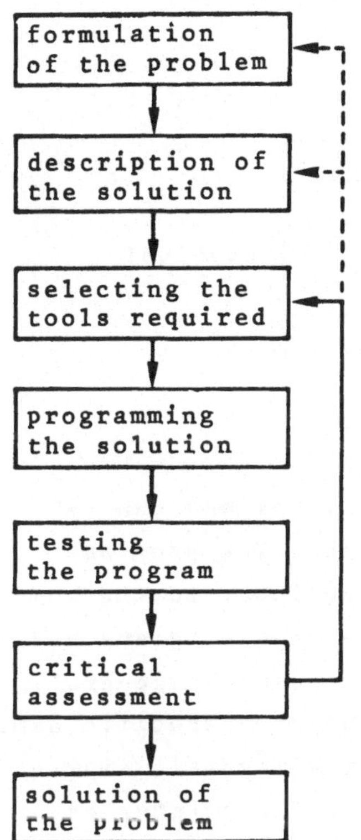

If, out of the different means
available, one decides to use a
computer then the solution has to be
written in a precise manner. Furthermore, all possible special cases
have to be recognized and taken into account. Only then can the solution path, for instance, in the
language Fortran, be programmed.

After the program has been prepared
in detail (at the office desk) the
sequence of statements can then be
input to the computer by, for
example, a terminal.

The computer accepts the program
which is formulated in a so-called
problem-oriented language. It then
translates the individual statements
with the aid of a special program,
the so-called compiler, into a lan-
guage which can be directly understood by the machine ("machine-
oriented language"). It is at this stage that the computer
recognized all offences against the rules of the problem-oriented
language and informs the programmer.

After the program has been tested, i.e. all formal errors have
been removed and the program supplies the calculated values,
the results have to be subject to a critical assessment. This
assessment determines whether

- the solution should be written in another manner,
- the means used should be changed

or   - the problem should be formulated in another way.

It is only after obtaining the desired results that the
problem under consideration can be thought of as being solved.

The particular configuration of the computer being used has no
significant effect on the formal structure of the programming
language Fortran. However, for general information it is advisable to know something about the arrangement of the computer
system. The following diagram is designed to illustrate this.

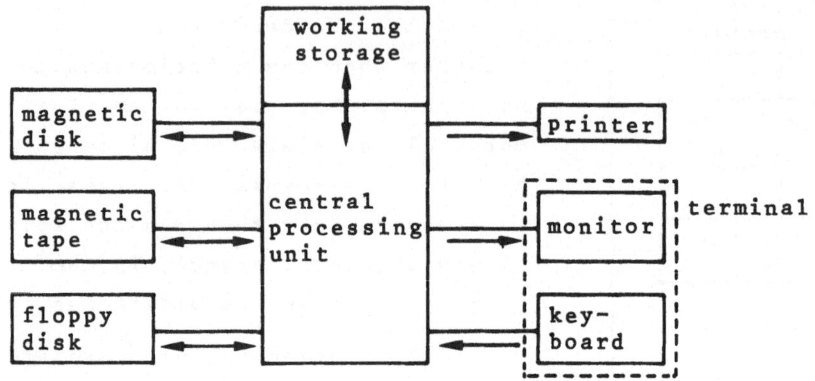

The central processing unit operates all devices and can be
thought of as being the heart of the computer. The programs
(and if necessary corresponding data) can be input to the computer by means of the keyboard. At the same time programs can
be displayed on a terminal for checking purposes. In general,
the sequence of the statements are stored under a specific name
on either a floppy disk, a magnetic tape or a magnetic disk and
are thus available for use at a later stage. The printer can
be used for the output of a list of programming statements,
for documentation purposes, or to list the results of a program
which has been executed.

The program remains in the working storage for the total duration
of the execution and, furthermore, all storage places required
by the program are reserved here.

The above diagram applies, on the one hand, to large computer
systems which are in a position to process a great number of
user programs at the same time and, on the other hand, to small
computers that are only used by one user ("personal computer").

Fortran 77 is designed as a uniform programming language capable
solving different problems independent of the particular
computer being used. As there is a considerable difference between the performance of large computer systems on the one hand,

and small systems on the other hand, a modified language of the
full language Fortran 77, namely Fortran 77 subset, has been
developed.

With respect to the interchangeability of programs it would
certainly be desirable if all programs were kept in two
groups according to the definition of the standards. Reality
shows, however, that the computer manufacturers offer various
extensions of the language Fortran 77 in order to exploit the
different possibilities of their computers to a maximum. If
and to what extent use is made of the language extension in a
program, depends on whether the program is to be used on a
different computer. In general, it is recommended to adhere
to the language standard as much as possible, i.e. if possible
not to exploit language extensions.

Fortran 77 is capable of dealing with variables and constants,
having different characteristics, which include

> - integer items   (INTEGER)
> - real items   (REAL and DOUBLE PRECISION)
> - complex items   (COMPLEX)
> - logical items   (LOGICAL)
> - character items   (CHARACTER)

DOUBLE PRECISION and COMPLEX data types are not available in
Fortran 77 subset.

The individual basic elements can be connected to form larger
units (e.g. arithmetic expressions, Boolean expressions,
character expressions), their values can be obtained as an output (WRITE statement) or values can be transferred to the
variables by means of assignment or input statements (READ)
from external storage devices.

Over and above this, a program can be structured using loops,
subprograms and also blocks. The various language elements will
be described using simple examples in the following chapters.
In doing so the aim is not to provide a complete description
of the language - this can be obtained in the handbooks -
but rather to provide an understanding of the language. [*)]

_____

[*)] Nevertheless, apart from a few statements that are hardly ever
used in practice, all Fortran 77 instructions have been
described; cf. Appendix D.

1 A Simple Example

In this chapter we will calculate the mean value m of two numbers a and b with the aid of a computer.

$$m = \frac{a+b}{2} \qquad a = 1.4, \qquad b = 2.1$$

If the above problem is solved mentally, the value 1.75 is obtained. The problem is, therefore, not to determine the value of m, but how the problem can be written in Fortran, i.e. "programmed". The program will first of all be presented and then explained.

Example 1.1

```
      REAL A,B,M
      A = 1.4
      B = 2.1
      M = (A+B)/2.0
      WRITE (*,100) A,B,M
  100 FORMAT (1X,5F15.6)
      STOP
      END
```

The "declaration statement"

```
      REAL A,B,M
```

requests 3 storage places for the names A, B and M, respectively. Since, in the course of the program, contents of the storage places can change, we do not in general use the term "storage places" but rather "variables" which possess a certain type - here REAL. The form in which the numbers are stored in the variables is thus defined and this, in turn, determines the range of numbers which the values can be taken from. It is here that the properties of the computer being used play a role (cf. Appendix A).

Names of the variables can, to a certain extent, be freely chosen: The first character must be a letter and this can then be followed by letters and digits in any particular sequence.[*] The maximum permissible length of a variable name is not allowed to exceed 6 characters in the standard language. There

[*] "letters" refers to all upper case letters A,B,...Z. The dollar sign ($) used to be considered the same as letter. This still applies to some computers today (e.g. Fujitsu, IBM, Siemens) even though it does not correspond to the standard Fortran 77.

are compilers which do, however, allow greater numbers of characters, but this possibility should not be taken advantage of, since this does not represent any significant extension, quite the opposite in that it makes it more difficult when trying to run the same program on different computers.

It is quite obvious that the variables chosen (or other items defined at a later point), should have different names and, furthermore, they should not coincide with the predefined names of the language, i.e. "key words" such as, for example, WRITE or END.

The variables are assigned to their places in the working storage; where this is exactly is unimportant for our purposes: The variable can be unequivocally identified by means of its name. What is important for us, however, is that the previous contents of the storage places are not deleted with the declaration statement: Initially the storage places contain the value which was defined in the previous program; we thus have to make sure that the old values are deleted and that the variables A and B receive the values 1.4 and 2.1. This takes place by means of the following two value assignments:

```
A = 1.4
B = 2.1
```

The value 1.4 is encoded in "floating point representation" in the variable A as described in Appendix A. In a similar manner the storage place B contains the value 2.1 in "floating point representation".

The arithmetical expression can now be programmed for the calculation of the mean value m.

```
M = (A+B)/2.0
```

The above statement can be interpreted as follows:

The contents of the storage places A and B are called up and added. The expression in parentheses is calculated. The intermediate result (=3.5) is divided by 2 (=1.75). The final result is assigned to the variable having the name M. In doing so the storage places A and B remain unchanged.

It is not only desired to calculate the value of M, but to print it together with A and B. This requires use of the following statements which will be explained in detail later.

```
     WRITE (*,100) A,B,M
 100 FORMAT (1X,5F15.6)
```

At this stage it should be noted that after the key word

```
     WRITE (*,100)
```

the names of the variables to be printed have to be separated by commas. There are no limitations to the length of the "list" of variables. The manner in which the values are printed is determined by the FORMAT statement.[*)] This will be dealt with in detail at a later stage. For the time being, however, all print statements for the output of variables having the type REAL will be written in this standard form.

Our program is ended - as is every other Fortran program - by means of the statement

```
     STOP
```

The statement

```
     END
```

informs the compiler that the program (in more general terms: segment of the program) is finished; it must, therefore, be the last statement of a program.

After presenting the program for the calculation of the mean value of two numbers and then providing an explanation, it is now necessary to describe how the program is input to the computer.

In the past, punch cards were used for years to input programs. Even though today input to a computer takes place by means of a keyboard - the results of the input being shown on a terminal -

---

[*)]
a) The * in the WRITE statement results in the output appearing on a predefined output device. In general, this is the printer, but it can also be a monitor. However, instead of * , an integer can be used for the device number. Traditionally the number 6 refers to the printer.
b) The FORMAT statement does not have to immediately follow the WRITE statement:
By means of the number 100 - in general the format number - a link is created between the WRITE and the FORMAT statements.

program input lines are arranged in exactly the same manner as the punch cards of the past.

A program line thus consists of 80 characters which correspond to the 80 columns of a punch card and, as a result, one often speaks of the "columns" in a program line but what is actually meant is the "positions" in the line.

Positions 7 to 72 are of special interest for the case of a Fortran program line: It is in this field that the statements required have to be written. Moreover, every statement must begin with a new program line. If the field is not long enough, for example the statement contains more than 66 characters, then the statement can be continued in a continuation line (from positions 7 to 72 [*]). In order to do this, the continuation line has to be marked with a character in position 6 which is, however, not equal to zero ("0"). The positions 1 - 5 can be used for numbers (consisting of the digits 0, 1,...,9) which represent the number of a statement. Statement numbers can be chosen at will; however, they must not coincide with other statement numbers in the program. For instance, in Example 1.1 the format statement has the number 100. There are no restrictions on the manner in which the statement number is entered in the first 5 columns, [**] however, for reasons of orderly programming, the user should make a habit of writing the number in a "right-aligned" manner, i.e. it should end in the last position (5).

The positions 73-80 can be used for numbering the sequence of the program lines. This was particularly important when using punch cards: The numbers enabled the user to recognize immediately if the cards were out of order. It is, however, impossible to mix up the input lines with the latest input devices. On the other hand, it is possible that the user mistakenly continues with a statement after position 72. This then leads to a program error, because the Fortran compiler does not recognize information between the positions 73 and 80.

---

[*] Up to 19 consecutive program lines are allowed in full Fortran 77 and up to 9 in the subset.

[**] For example, the following can be written:

```
1    0 0
position: 1      5
```

In Fortran, the program line thus has the following structure:

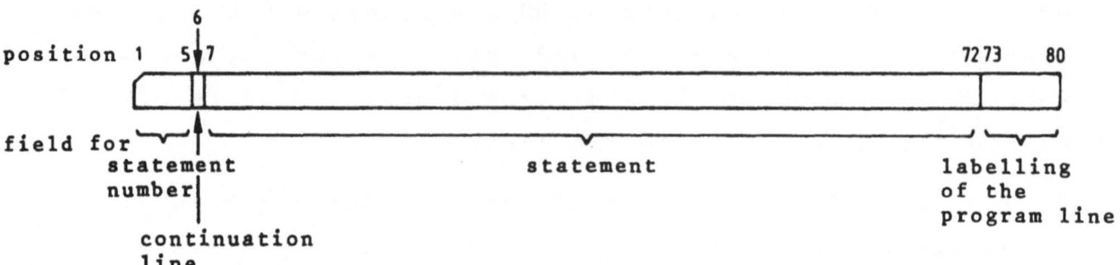

In order to make it easier for other people to read and analyze
the statements of a program, comment lines can be included at
any point. These are characterized by the letter C or the
character * (asterisk) in the first position of the program
line. The compiler considers the comment line to be analogue
to an empty line, i.e. an input line which contains no characters, at least in the field from position 1 - 72, and as a
result ignores it.

The explanations provided above are sufficient for the input of
the program in Example 1.1. However, it is not only necessary
to input the Fortran statements: The computer has to be informed
that it is dealing with a job and the compiler has to be called.
As these so-called control statements differ according to the
computer, they will only be schematically illustrated here in
order to show how the Fortran statements are integrated into
the complete program:

   job-identification

   calling of the compiler

      Fortran statements

   additional job control statements to execute the program
   if necessary

When dealing with personal computers the necessary information
for controlling a program can often be input by means of a
man - machine dialogue.

Exercise 1.1

Input the program given in Example 1.1 in a computer
so that it runs.

Exercise 1.2

The area F of a triangle having sides a, b, c is given by

$$F = \sqrt{s(s-a)(s-b)(s-c)} \qquad \text{with } s = \frac{a+b+c}{2}$$

Write a program that is capable of calculating the area
of a triangle having sides a = 2, b = 3.5 and c = 4.
Output the results.

Hint: 1) Use the character ∗ for multiplication.

2) Instead of the square root sign $\sqrt{}$, the exponentiation $(...)^{0.5}$ can be chosen whereby the exponent is
placed after the double character ∗∗ .

2 The Formation of Arithmetic Expressions

The previous chapter dealt with variables of the type REAL.
These variables are used for storing real numbers ("floating
point numbers"). If certain tasks require integer (positive or
negative) values to be stored in the variables, then this can
be carried out using the type INTEGER. The variable names
separated by commas are then listed after the key word INTEGER.
The method of storage is described in Appendix A.

Not only variables, but also constants can be defined using
different types; if a constant - not taking into account the
sign - consists of a sequence of digits, then it represents an
integer or it is what is called an INTEGER constant. A negative
constant is characterized by the minus sign (-) in front of the
sequence of digits; if desired, a plus sign (+) may be placed
before a sequence of digits for a positive number but it is not
absolutely necessary.

A REAL constant consists not only of the sign and sequence of
digits but also of a decimal point. The decimal point can be
placed in front of, in the middle of, or after a sequence of
digits according to the value under consideration. The following
are some examples of REAL constants:

$$1.3 \quad -.7 \quad 2. \quad + 128.0$$

It should be noted that 2. as well as 128.0 are REAL constants,
since they both possess a decimal point, even though their
values are identical to an integer number.[*)]

The values of REAL constants can often be spread over a large
range of numbers, and it is, therefore, often inconvenient to
write the values in the manner described above. Numbers can,
however, be transformed as follows:

$$1273 = 1.273 \cdot 10^3 = 12.73 \cdot 10^2$$

or

$$0.0001273 = 1.273 \cdot 10^{-4} = 0.01273 \cdot 10^{-2}$$

It is possible in Fortran to write constants in a similar
manner, whereby the basis 10 is replaced by the letter E
(for exponent):

[*)] Attention to this difference is important with respect to the
evaluation of arithmetic expressions, cf. pages 12 and 111.

```
For          1273:        1.273E3        12.73E+2
        0.0001273:        1.273E-4       0.01273E-2
```

Thus in a Fortran program a REAL constant has the following general form:[*)]

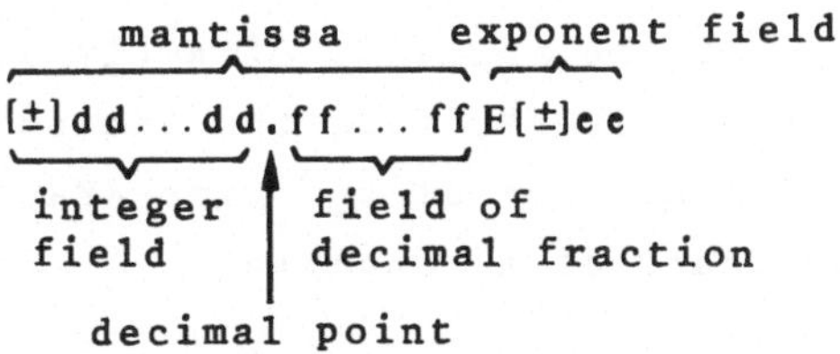

In this general form it is allowed to omit either the decimal point or the exponent field. Furthermore, either the integer field or the field of the decimal fraction may be empty (not, however, both at the same time). Hence

```
    1273.          .1273E4          1273E0
```

are permissible representations of the REAL constant having the value 1273.0.

A combination of

        INTEGER variable
        INTEGER constant
        REAL variable
        REAL constant

and arithmetic operators enable all kinds of complicated arithmetic expressions to be formulated. The following operators are available:

Sign	Meaning	Priority
**	exponentiation	1
*	multiplication	2
/	division	
+	addition	3
-	subtraction	

In addition, special characters such as the parentheses (and) are allowed to fix the sequence of evaluation.

____

[*)] The number of significant digits depends on the computer being used; if more digits are written in the program, the internal precision does not increase (cf. page 15 and Appendix A).

A given arithmetic expression is thus reduced in steps so that
two operands connected by means of an operator lead to an
intermediate result. The sequence in which the pairs of
operands are processed depends on the priority of the operator
(see above). The type of the different intermediate results is
determined by the type of the operands directly used. If both
operands are of the type INTEGER, then the intermediate result
is of the type INTEGER otherwise of the type REAL. This will
now be illustrated by means of an example.

Example 2.1

```
REAL W,A,B
INTEGER N
N = 4
A = 3.5
B = 1.5
W = 7/N*(A+B)-B**2/3
. . .
```

The operators / and $*$ of the first partial expression $7/N*(A+B)$
have the same priorities and as a result the arithmetic
expression is processed in a "left to right" manner and the
first expression to be calculated is

$$7/N$$

The intermediate result is stored in an auxiliary variable z_1.
The auxiliary variable z_1 is of the type INTEGER, because 7 is
an INTEGER constant and N is an INTEGER variable. The calculated
value $7/N = 1.75$ is truncated so that the intermediate
result is

$$z_1 = 1$$

The arithmetic expression is thus reduced to

$$z_1*(A+B)-B**2/3$$

The next step is to evaluate the expression A+B which is given
in parentheses:

$$z_2 = (A+B)$$
$$= 5.0$$

whereby the auxiliary variable z_2 is of the type REAL. The
expression is thus reduced to

$$z_1*z_2-B**2/3$$

The two auxiliary variables z_1 and z_2 are now multiplied with one another.

$$z_3 = z_1 \star z_2$$
$$= 5.0$$

The auxiliary variable z_3 is of the type REAL, because z_2 is of this type.

The arithmetic expression is thus reduced to

$$z_3 - B \star\star 2/3$$

Since exponentiation has the highest priority, the following calculation is carried out next:

$$z_4 = B \star\star 2$$
$$= 2.25 \qquad (z_4 : \text{Type REAL because of B})$$

The arithmetic expression is now:

$$z_3 - z_4/3$$

As division has a higher priority than subtraction, it is the next calculation to be carried out:

$$z_5 = z_4/3$$
$$= 0.75 \qquad (z_5 : \text{Type REAL because of } z_4)$$

We thus obtain the reduced arithmetic expression

$$z_3 - z_5$$

which then has to be evaluated as:

$$z_6 = z_3 - z_5$$
$$= 4.25$$

Due to the statement (see above)

$$W = \ldots$$

the value is then assigned to the variable W.

When evaluating the arithmetic expressions the following rules were applied:

1) Multiplication and division have priority over addition and subtraction.

2) If the operations have the same priority (multiplication and
division, addition and subtraction) then those operations
to the left are executed first.

Furthermore the following also applies:

3) If a number of exponentiations directly follow one another,
then that exponentiation which is the furthest to be right
is carried out first.[*]

It is quite obvious that the sequence of evaluation plays a
significant role in determining the result of an arithmetic
expression: If this sequence is not adhered to, then this
can lead to the following:

- the permissible range of numbers can be exceeded for
  the case of intermediate results,
- intermediate results can be subject to a higher
  degree of inaccuracy,
- the intermediate result can be zero.

In this respect the following exercise should serve as an
example:

Exercise 2.1

What values do the variables possess after processing
the following program segment, if the number representation described in Appendix A is applied?

```
REAL A,B,C,D
INTEGER J,K,N
K = 12345        ◄────────    ⎡ alternative K = 1234567890
J = 10                        ⎣ when using a main frame computer
A = J**(-2)
B = J**(-2.)
C = K*5/J
D = K*(5/J)
N = (K+0.)*5/J
```

Hint: Extend the given statements to a complete program and
print the calculated values. How should the results be
interpreted?

---

[*] Hence a**b**c is the same as a**(b**c). However, for reasons
of clarity, it is recommended to use parentheses.

The accuracy provided by the number representation for constants and variables of the type REAL is often not sufficient for certain problems. This can be the case for long arithmetic expressions or more complex calculations. As a result, full Fortran 77 (not, however, the subset) provides for an extra type of data, namely, constants and variables having the type

    DOUBLE PRECISION

If more than one variable of this type is required, then they have to be separated by commas after the two key words.[*)] The internal number representation is illustrated in Appendix A.

A "double precision" constant is written in a similar manner to a REAL constant, whereby the letter E which represents the exponent field is replaced by the letter D. Thus 1.273D-2 represents the number 0.01273 in the "double precision" storage form.

In the case of some compilers it used to be possible to achieve the storage form DOUBLE PRECISION by means of a sufficiently large number of digits. This possibility is not provided for in the new standard Fortran 77: If too many digits are given, this does not increase the accuracy, they are simply rounded off. Hence (for the case of a computer having 6 digit accuracy for REAL) the constant

    3.141592653 is different from the number
    3.141592653D0

(The first constant is rounded to 3.14159).

A mixing of items having types REAL and DOUBLE PRECISION is allowed in arithmetic expressions, but should, however, be avoided. If a particular problem under consideration requires DOUBLE PRECISION, then all real value items should be declared as DOUBLE PRECISION. Rounding errors can very easily occur in mixed expressions and these are extremely difficult to locate. In addition, the main reasons for mixed expressions (a shortening of the computing time, a reduction in working storage requirements) are relatively insignificant today.

[*)] Apart from the key words DOUBLE PRECISION, some compilers can also use the key word REAL*8. This should, however, not be taken advantage of as it is not included in standard Fortran 77.

3 Loop Control, Logical Items

The previous chapter described a very simple program structure:
Values were calculated and printed using some variables and
constants. Finally the program was terminated. The advantages
of a computer can, however, first be exploited when, in the
course of the program, branching can be carried out depending
on the values determined. Thus, certain program segments can be
repeated a number of times. Fortran provides language elements
for this purpose which will now be illustrated and explained
by means of the following example.

Example 3.1

Calculate and print the value of the polynomial

$$y = 2x^2 + 3x - 1$$

for the interval $[-1, 1.5]$ using a step length of 0.1

```
      REAL X,Y
      X = -1.0
    1 Y = 2.0*X**2+3.0*X-1.0
      WRITE (*,100) X,Y
  100 FORMAT (1X,5F15.6)
      X = X+0.1
      IF (X .LE. 1.5) GO TO 1
      STOP
      END
```

In the program solution illustrated above, the statements are
executed as follows:

- Storage places are reserved for the two variables
  X and Y.
- The variable X is assigned the value -1.0.
- The arithmetic expression 2.0*X**2+3.0*X-1.0 is eva-
  luated for the value X = -1.0 and assigned to Y.
- The values of X and Y are printed according to the
  format defined.

The statement

      X = X+0.1

is then executed. As the above expression is, at first glance,
a little confusing, we shall now consider it in more detail:
On the right-hand side of the assignment sign (=) we have the
arithmetical expression

    X+0.1

which has now to be evaluated. Now, since the value -1.0 is
stored in the variable X, then X+0.1 results in the arithmetic
expression having the value -0.9. This value is assigned to the
variable X due to the statement

    X = ...

Thus the old value (= -1.0) of the variable is replaced by the
new value (= -0.9). It is also said that the statement

    X = X+0.1

increases the contents of X by 0.1.

The final statement

    GO TO 1

is a skip statement which says that the program execution has
to be continued at the statement number 1. Our program, therefore, branches back to the statement

    1 Y = 2.0*X**2+3.0*X-1.0

and the arithmetic expression is evaluated for the value
X = -0.9. The result is then assigned to the variable Y and
printed together with the value of X. Since it is only required
to evaluate the value of the polynomial y up to the upper
limit 1.5, the return will only continue as long as the variable

    "X is less than or equal to 1.5"
applies. As a result the following programming statement was
made:

    IF (X .LE. 1.5) GO TO 1

The above statement is a so-called logical IF statement which
has the general form

    IF (le) s

whereby

    le   stands for a logical expression and
    s   stands for the statement to be executed.

In our example the logical IF-statement consisted of a skip command.[*] However, in general, any kind of statement which we wish to execute can be inserted at this point. The logical expression le was the arithmetic comparison in our programming example:

$$X \leq 1.5 \qquad \text{or in Fortran} \qquad X \text{ .LE. } 1.5$$

The following comparisons can be made between items of the type REAL, DOUBLE PRECISION or INTEGER.

Mathematical Sign	Comparison Operator	Meaning
$<$	.LT.	less than
$\leq$	.LE.	less than or equal to
$=$	.EQ.	equal to
$\geq$	.GE.	greater than or equal to
$>$	.GT.	greater than
$\neq$	.NE.	not equal

Arithmetic expressions are allowed on both sides of the comparison operator for the case of an arithmetic comparison, and furthermore they are allowed to have different types: The arithmetic expressions are evaluated individually and one of the items may be transformed into the type of the other item. (INTEGER $\longrightarrow$ REAL $\longrightarrow$ DOUBLE PRECISION)[**]

Thus the comparison

        a .LT. b

between two arithmetic expressions results in the value "true" if a is less than b and otherwise in the value "false". Corresponding results are obtained for the other comparison operators. The logical IF statement

        IF (le) s

---

[*] The general form of the skip command is
        GOTO m
where m represents a statement number. The program continues with that statement which has the number m.

[**] One should be aware that this can result in a loss of accuracy (INTEGER $\longrightarrow$ REAL), and by no means an increase in accuracy (REAL $\longrightarrow$ DOUBLE PRECISION).

executes the statement s only if the logical expression le has the value "true". If this does not apply, then the program continues with the next statement.

In the solution to Example 3.1, the program is ended with the statement

    STOP

if the comparison

    X .LE. 1.5

results in the value "false", i.e. if the value of the variable X is greater than 1.5.

The programming language Fortran enables logical values to be stored in variables having the type LOGICAL. The names of the variables have to be declared after the key word

    LOGICAL

and have to be separated by commas.

Variables can be connected to logical expressions with the aid of logical operators in a similar manner to arithmetic expressions. Fortran is capable of dealing with the following logical operators:

Mathematical Sign	Logical Operator	Priority	
$\neg$	.NOT.	1	
$\wedge$	.AND.	2	
$\vee$	.OR.	3	
$\equiv$	.EQV.	4	not included in subset Fortran
$\neq$	.NEQV.		

The sequence of evaluation which is applied when reducing a logical expression depends on the priority of respective operators directly used. In addition, pairs of parentheses may be used in order to produce a different sequence of evaluation. The values necessary for the connection of the two logical variables a and b are given by the following table whereby T stands for .TRUE. and F for .FALSE. [*)]

$$.NOT.\ a \ = \ \begin{cases} T & \text{if a has the value .FALSE.} \\ F & \text{if a has the value .TRUE.} \end{cases}$$

<table>
<tr><td colspan="3">a .AND. b</td><td></td><td colspan="3">a .OR. b</td><td></td><td colspan="3">a .EQV. b</td><td></td><td colspan="3">a .NEQV. b</td></tr>
<tr><td>a\b</td><td>T</td><td>F</td><td></td><td>a\b</td><td>T</td><td>F</td><td></td><td>a\b</td><td>T</td><td>F</td><td></td><td>a\b</td><td>T</td><td>F</td></tr>
<tr><td>T</td><td>T</td><td>F</td><td></td><td>T</td><td>T</td><td>T</td><td></td><td>T</td><td>T</td><td>F</td><td></td><td>T</td><td>F</td><td>T</td></tr>
<tr><td>F</td><td>F</td><td>F</td><td></td><td>F</td><td>T</td><td>F</td><td></td><td>F</td><td>F</td><td>T</td><td></td><td>F</td><td>T</td><td>F</td></tr>
</table>

A short example will now be presented in order to make clear the application of logical items:

Example 3.2

```
REAL X1, Y1, X2, Y2, X, Y
LOGICAL A, INTX, INTY
X1 = 1.5
X2 = 6.3
Y1 = 3.2
Y2 = 6.8
X  = . . .]
Y  = . . .]  ←——————— X and Y are assigned arbitrary values
INTX = (X .GT. X1) .AND. (X .LT. X2)
INTY = (Y .GT. Y1) .AND. (Y .LT. Y2)
A = INTX .AND. INTY
```

The variable A possesses the value .TRUE., if the point (X, Y) lies in the shaded rectangle shown below. On the other hand, the variable A possesses the value .FALSE., if the point lies on the boundary of the rectangle or outside it.

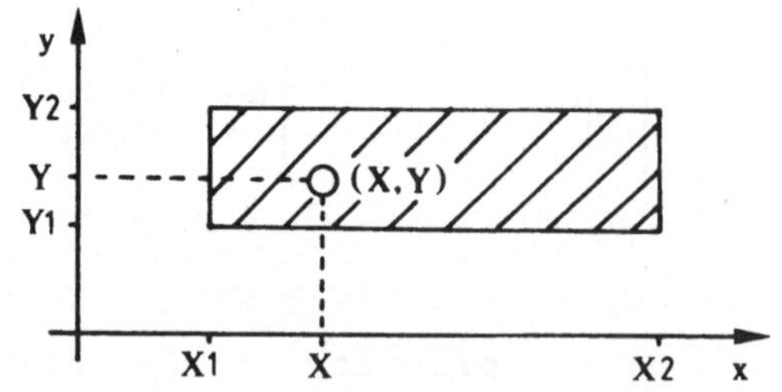

[*)] The items .TRUE. and .FALSE. represent the two logical constants. They can also be used in this form in the Fortran program, for instance in a value assignment to a logical variable A:
```
     A = .TRUE.
```

Apart from the logical IF statement, the arithmetic IF statement can be used for branching depending on the arithmetic value used.[*] It has the general form:

    IF (ae) n_1,n_2,n_3

where ae   is an arithmetic expression and

$\left.\begin{array}{l} n_1 \\ n_2 \\ n_3 \end{array}\right]$ stand for 3 statement numbers (which do not necessarily have to be different from one another).

If the arithmetic expression ae

- is negative, then the program branches to the statement having the number n_1,
- is zero, then the program branches to the statement having the number n_2,
- is positive, then the program branches to the statement having the number n_3.

The logical IF statement has the disadvantage that only a single statement, which is dependent on the logical expression, can be executed (cf. page 17). If two or more statements are to be dependent on a condition, then the sequence of statements has to be made at a special position in the program. The program then has to jump to this particular position by means of a logical IF statement and finally return. This extra skip instruction results in the program becoming a lot more diffi-cult to follow. This can, however, be avoided in Fortran 77 by using the statements

    IF (le) THEN
    ELSE
    END IF

and furthermore

    ELSE IF (le) THEN

---

[*] In the initial stages of Fortran programming, the arithmetic IF statement was the only possibility for branching. - A program becomes very difficult to follow if there are a lot of skip statements and arithmetic IF statements. They should thus be avoided if possible. In some cases it is better to use the block IF-statement.

As a result, the series of statements are grouped together to form a unit or a block. Therefore, in general we speak of a block IF statement which can have various forms.

<u>First form:</u> Execution of the statements $s_1,\ldots,s_k$ as a result of the logical expression le.

Using the newly introduced statements	Using statements already known
IF (le) THEN	IF (.NOT. le) GOTO m_1
$\quad s_1$	$\quad s_1$
$\quad \ldots$	$\quad \ldots$
$\quad s_k$	$\quad s_k$
END IF	m_1 CONTINUE $\qquad$ *)

If the logical expression le possesses the value .TRUE., then the sequence of statements $s_1,\ldots,s_k$ is executed.

<u>Second form:</u> An alternative execution of the statements $s_{11},\ldots,s_{1k_1}$ and $s_{21},\ldots,s_{2k_2}$ resulting from the logical expression le.

IF (le) THEN	IF (.NOT. le) GOTO m_1
$\quad s_{11}$	$\quad s_{11}$
$\quad \ldots$	$\quad \ldots$
$\quad s_{1k_1}$	$\quad s_{1k_1}$
	$\quad$ GOTO m_2
ELSE	m_1 CONTINUE
$\quad s_{21}$	$\quad s_{21}$
$\quad \ldots$	$\quad \ldots$
$\quad s_{2k_2}$	$\quad s_{2k_2}$
END IF	m_2 CONTINUE

If the logical expression le possesses the value .TRUE., then the sequence of statements $s_{11},\ldots,s_{1k_1}$ will be executed and the sequence $s_{21},\ldots,s_{2k_2}$ will be skipped. If, on the other hand, it possesses the value .FALSE., then the statements $s_{11},\ldots,s_{1k_1}$ will be skipped and the statements $s_{21},\ldots,s_{2k_2}$ will be executed. In both cases the statement following the END IF will be executed.

---

*) The statement CONTINUE has no meaning; it is simply used for statement numbers to be skipped to or for the end of a loop.

<u>Third form</u>: To distinguish between different cases using logical expressions le_1, $le_2, \ldots, le_n$.

IF (le_1) THEN	IF (.NOT. le_1) GOTO m_1
s_{11}	s_{11}
...	...
s_{1k_1}	s_{1k_1}
	GOTO m
ELSE IF (le_2) THEN	m_1 IF (.NOT. le_2) GOTO m_2
s_{21}	s_{21}
...	...
s_{2k_2}	s_{2k_2}
	GOTO m
ELSE IF (le_3) THEN	m_2 IF (.NOT. le_3) GOTO m_3
s_{31}	s_{31}
...	...
s_{3k_3}	s_{3k_3}
	GOTO m
...	m_3 ...
ELSE IF (le_n) THEN	m_{n-1} IF (.NOT. le_n) GOTO m
s_{n1}	s_{n1}
...	...
s_{nk_n}	s_{nk_n}
END IF	m CONTINUE

If the first logical expression le_1 possesses the value .TRUE., then the sequence of statements $s_1, \ldots, s_{1k_1}$ will be carried out and the program will then be continued at the statement following the above END IF statement.

If, however, the logical expression le_1 possesses the value .FALSE., then the sequence of statements $s_{11}, \ldots, s_{1k_1}$ will be skipped and the logical expression le_2 evaluated in the first ELSE statement. If it possesses the value .TRUE., then the sequence of statements $s_{21}, \ldots, s_{2k_2}$ will be executed and the program will be finally continued after the END IF statement. If it possesses the value .FALSE., then the sequence of statements $s_{21}, \ldots, s_{2k_2}$ will be skipped and the program branches to the next ELSE IF statement. The remaining ELSE IF statements are processed in a similar manner.

Each of the statements s_k is allowed to be any of the three
forms of the block IF statement so that the block IF statements
can be nested within one another. In order to make quite clear
to the reader that the statements are dependent on the logical
expressions, they can, as indicated above, be indented slightly. The advantages of this method will be recognized when we
deal with more complex problems (cf. for example the solution
to Exercise 9.1).

The control of loops by means of IF statements becomes difficult when a number of loops are nested within each other. We
shall, therefore, now explain the DO-loop which has the following general form:

```
DO n   d = a,e,i
   s
    1
   ...
   s
    k
n CONTINUE
```

where n stands for the statement number,
      d stands for the DO-variable
      a stands for initial value,
      e stands for the final value and
      i stands for the increment
      $s_1,\ldots,s_k$ stand for the sequence of statements to be
                 repeatedly executed.

The DO-loop is valid from the DO statement up to and including
the statement having the number n.[*]

The full Fortran 77 permits the initial value a, the final
value e and the increment i to be arithmetic expressions of
the type INTEGER, DOUBLE PRECISION or REAL (they may not, however, be changed within the DO-loop), whilst the subset version
only allows for INTEGER constants or INTEGER variables. As a
result of this difference, the DO-variable in the subset is
only allowed to be a variable of the type INTEGER, whilst in full
Fortran 77 it may also possess the type REAL or DOUBLE PRECISION.

---

[*] The statement having the number n does not have to be a
CONTINUE statement, instead it can be any executable statement.
However, since there are a number of exceptions and as DO-loops
can be nested, it is recommended to use the additional CONTINUE
statement.

The execution of the DO-loop can be thought of as taking place as follows: [*]

1) The DO-variable d is assigned the initial value a.
2) The computer checks if the DO-variable has exceeded the final value e.
   a) If the final value e has not been exceeded, then all statements contained within the DO-loop up to the statement having the number n are executed.
   b) If the final value e has been exceeded, then the program leaves the DO loop and continues with the statement that follows the statement having the number n.
3) The DO-variable d is increased by the increment i and then the program branches back to point 2.

Since the items a, e and i are allowed to be variables or, in full Fortran 77, even arithmetic expressions, it is possible that the final condition is fulfilled from the very beginning. If this is the case, the program does not even go once through the DO-loop, since the test described under point 2 above is carried out before the loop is entered. [**]

<u>Exercise 3.1</u>

   a) Using Example 3.1 find a solution using the DO-loop.

   b) How can the program be written in the subset when the items of the DO-statement are only allowed to be integer values?

When determining the zero points of a function f(x) it is frequently impossible to give the zero positions in an arithmethic expression. This problem can, however, be overcome by the use of a formula $\varphi(x)$ which, starting from an initial value, provides approximate values which are then improved on to reach the desired zero position ("iteration method").

$$x_{j+1} := \varphi(x_j) \qquad j = o, 1, \ldots$$

---

[*] a) For further details cf. Appendix B.
b) It is initially assumed that the step length i is positive.

[**] In standard Fortran IV, the test is carried out at the end of the DO-loop. The DO-loop is thus processed at least once (cf. Appendix B).

A zero position of the function $f(x)$ is determined when the iteration method being used is "stationary", i.e. repeatedly provides the same value (fixed point).

$$\bar{x} = \varphi(\bar{x}) \longleftrightarrow f(\bar{x}) = 0$$

It can thus be proved that the sequence of values x_j converge to a fixed point $\bar{x}$ if the functions $f(x)$ or $\varphi(x)$ fulfill certain conditions.[*)]

The case can, however, occur that even when convergence conditions are present, the sequence of the values x_j converges too slowly. Rounding errors can then have such a strong influence that the sequence of values does not converge to the desired fixed point $\bar{x}$. Hence, before using certain iteration methods, the user should look at the mathematical model in detail in order to assure himself that the method will quickly converge. It is recommended to place a counter in the iteration loop used to determine the fixed point in order to establish how often the loop has been processed so that the method can be broken after, for instance, 10 runs.

The following exercise illustrates the application of the Newton iteration method.

$$x_{j+1} := \varphi(x_j) = x_j - \frac{f(x_j)}{f'(x_j)} \qquad j = 0, 1,\ldots$$

This method requires that the derivative f' is not equal to 0 in the interval, and as a result it should only be used to calculate simple zero positions of f.

<u>Exercise 3.2</u>

Calculate the zero position of the function $f(x) = x^2 - 3$ using the Newton iteration method.

<u>Hint:</u>

The method converges for x_o greater than 1.

[*)]For functions $\varphi(x)$ that can be differentiated, the condition $|\varphi(x)| \leqslant k < 1$ for example is adequate for the interval under consideration. For further details see for example H. Werner: Praktische Mathematik I, Berlin 1970.

4 Polynomials; Vectors, Matrices

In the previous chapter the function

$$y = 2 \cdot x^2 + 3 \cdot x - 1$$

was considered a number of times. The above function represents a polynomial of the second degree. In general polynomials have the form

$$y = \sum_{j=o}^{n} a_j \cdot x^j = a_o + a_1 x + a_2 x^2 + \ldots + a_{n-1} x^{n-1} + a_n x^n$$

If the coefficient a_n differs from 0, then n is called the degree of the polynomial.

The coefficients a_o, a_1,...,a_n can be combined to form a vector

$$A = (a_o, a_1, \ldots, a_n)$$

which is the so-called coefficient vector. It is obvious that the vector A describes the polynomial y.

By means of a declaration statement in the Fortran program it is possible to reserve storage space for a vector. In doing so, the name of the vector as well as the lower and upper limits of the index which are separated by a colon and given in paren- theses, [*)] have to be declared after one of the following key words

    DOUBLE PRECISION
    INTEGER
    LOGICAL
    REAL

It is only allowed to use constant integer values for the in- dex limits. Thus, the declaration statement for the coeffi- cient vector A - see above - must have the form

    REAL A(0:10)

whereby the degree of the polynomial n has always to be smaller or equal to 10. This declaration statement, therefore, reserves the following area in the working storage:

[*)] The lower limit of the index is set at 1 for Fortran IV and Fortran 77 subset; only the upper limit can be defined and has to be provided with an appropriate index shift (cf. page 115). REAL A(11) has then to be declared for the vector A.

Vector A 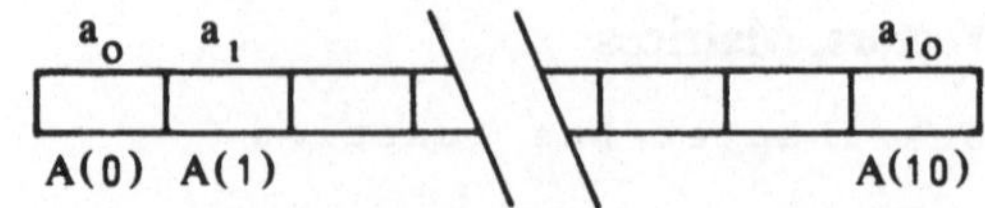

At a later stage in the program it is possible to access the individual components a_j of the vector A by means of A(j). The index j must be an arithmetic expression of the type INTEGER and must lie between 0 and 10. If an error is made and the given index is smaller than 0 or greater than 10, then no error message is reported and a storage place is called which lies before or after the vector A in the working storage.[*]

If we wish to declare more than one vector, then this can be done in a joint declaration statement with other variables of the same type, whereby the limits have to be separately declared for each vector.

Example 4.1

Calculate the function

$$y = 2x^2 + 3x - 1$$

as a general polynomial within the interval $[-1, 1.5]$ using a step length of 0.1.[**]

```
      REAL X,A(0:2),Y,S
      INTEGER K,N
      N = 2
      A(0) = -1
      A(1) =  3
      A(2) =  2
      DO 2 X = -1, 1.5, 0.1
      S = 0
      DO 1 K = N, 0, -1
      S = S*X+A(K)
    1 CONTINUE
      Y = S
      WRITE (*,100) X,Y
    2 CONTINUE
  100 FORMAT (1X,5F15.6)
      STOP
      END
```

[*] Some Fortran compilers provide for the option of supervising the index limits. This option should definitely be taken advantage of since such errors are usually very difficult to locate.

[**] The solution presented is possible in full Fortran 77 not, however, in the subset and Fortran IV; cf. an alternative solution on page 115.

The calculation of the values of the polynomial is based on
the so-called Horner Scheme. Since its application enables the
calculation to be carried out far more effectively than the
formula given on page 27, the Horner Scheme will now be briefly
explained. The initial formula is transformed and as many
factors x as possible are placed outside the parentheses:

$$y = \sum_{j=o}^{n} a_j x^j = a_o + a_1 x + a_2 x^2 + \ldots + a_n x^n$$

$$= a_n x^n + a_{n-1} x^{n-1} + \ldots + a_1 x + a_o$$

$$= (\ldots((a_n x + a_{n-1}) x + a_{n-2}) x + \ldots + a_1) x + a_o$$

Now if

$$
\begin{aligned}
s_{n+1} &:= 0 \\
s_n &:= a_n & &= s_{n+1} x + a_n \\
s_{n-1} &:= a_n x + a_{n-1} & &= s_n \cdot x + a_{n-1} \\
&\ldots & &\ldots \\
s_o &:= (\ldots(a_n x + a_{n-1}) x + \ldots + a_2) x + a_1) x + a_o & &= s_1 \cdot x + a_o
\end{aligned}
$$

then from the above it can be seen that s_o corresponds to the
transformed line of the polynomial y. The partial sums s_k are
given by the recursive formula

$$s_k = s_{k+1} \cdot x + a_k \qquad \text{for } k = n, n-1, \ldots, o$$

and the initial value $s_{n+1} = 0$.

Since every succeeding component s_k only requires the value s_{k+1}
which directly preceded it, every value can be overwritten using
its succeeding component, i.e. only one storage place S is required as shown in Example 4.1 above:

1) $S = 0$
2) $S = S \cdot x + a_k$ for $k = n, n-1, \ldots, o$
3) $y = S$

Since it is necessary to reserve one storage place for the
polynomial value y, the storage place S can also be saved by
using the variable y for the intermediate values, cf. solution,
page 115.

Fortran programs are not only capable of dealing with vectors, which can be considered as one-dimensional fields, but also with multi-dimensional matrices. In doing so the limiting values for every dimension have to be provided with the corresponding indices.[*] Full Fortran 77 allows for up to 7 dimensions, whilst the subset version allows only up to 3. If the matrix elements are called later in the program, then the individual index values have to be separated by commas. In addition, when dealing with matrices, the index values are not checked to see if they lie within the limits specified in the declaration.

<u>Example 4.2</u>

By means of the declaration

        INTEGER N,B(6,3),P1(0:5,-3:6,5)

the following items are declared:

1) A (simple) variable having the name N,
2) a two-dimensional matrix B, which possesses 6 x 3, i.e. 18 elements, and
3) a three-dimensional matrix P1 having 6 x 10 x 5, i.e. 300 elements.

The variable N and all elements of the two matrices B and P1 are of the type INTEGER. The elements of the matrix B can be called by means of

    B(i,j)   with $1 \leqslant i \leqslant 6$ and $1 \leqslant j \leqslant 3$

at a later point in the program (i,j: are arithmetic expressions having the type INTEGER).

Similarly for the three-dimensional matrix P1:

    P1(i,j,k)   with $0 \leqslant i \leqslant 5$, $-3 \leqslant j \leqslant 6$ and $1 \leqslant k \leqslant 5$

where i,j,k once again stand for arithmetic expressions of the type INTEGER.

Every (multidimensional) matrix is transformed internally into a vector with the individual columns of the matrix being stored one after the other:

---

[*] In both Fortran IV and the subset of Fortran 77 the lower limit is set at 1 and it is only necessary to define the upper limit. The following applies for full Fortran 77: If the lower limit is equal to 1, then it is only necessary to define the upper limit.

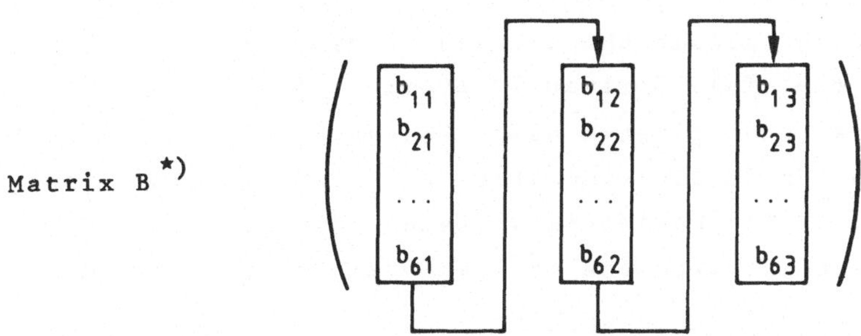

Matrix B [*)]

It is stored internally as follows

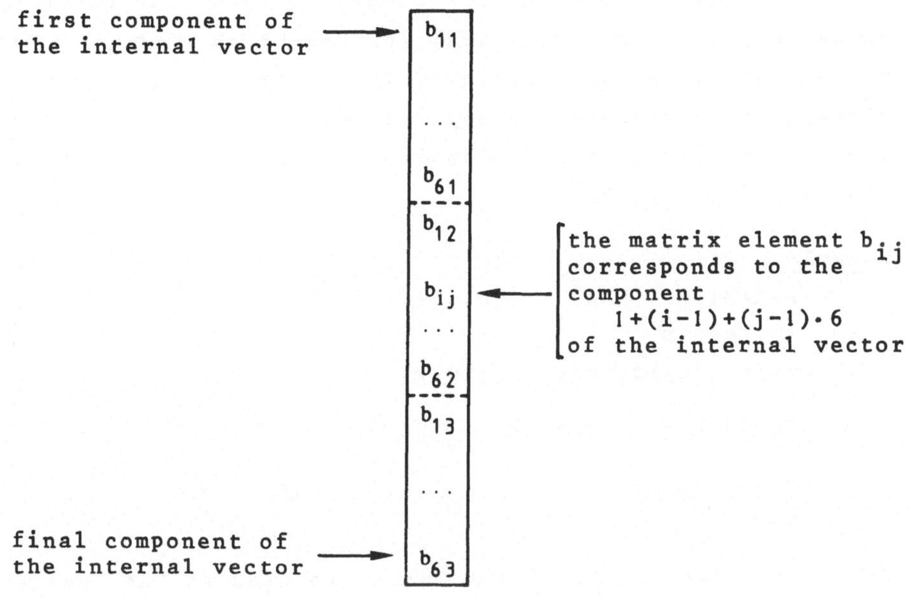

At every call of a matrix element, the computer automatically
calculates the corresponding component of the internal vector.
If, by mistake, the wrong index value of a matrix element is
used, for instance B(10,2), then the 16th component of the
internal vector will be called which corresponds to the matrix
element B(4,3). The program then continues its calculations
using this wrongly called element without registering an error.

If a program uses several fields having the same limits and
these limits are accessed at a later point in the program, then
program changes are very susceptible to errors: It is very

[*)] In mathematics, matrices are usually considered in rows (i.e.
the final index is dealt with quicker than the first one). This
difference requires careful attention.

easy to forget to include the changes everywhere. It is because of this that full Fortran 77 provides the possibility for
constant values to be given a name. The names of the constants
can be used in the declaration statements for the dimensions
of the fields. [*] The PARAMETER statement serves the purpose
of linking the names with the constant values. It has the
general form:

$$\text{PARAMETER } (n_1 = w_1 \ [,n_2 = w_2] \ \ldots)$$

where $n_1, n_2, \ldots$ represent the names for which the constant
values $w_1, w_2, \ldots$ are reserved. The PARAMETER statement has to
precede all other declarations. The names $n_1, n_2, \ldots$ are not
allowed to be repeated in any following declarations. Furthermore, it is not allowed to assign them any value in the later
course of the program.

<u>Example:</u>
```
      PARAMETER (NMAX = 100, PI = 3.1415926)
      INTEGER N
      REAL A(NMAX,NMAX), B(NMAX)
      ...
      DO 99 N = 1, NMAX,1
      ...
   99 CONTINUE
      ...
```

Very often the letters i,j,k,l,m,n are used as the indices for
the elements of vectors and matrices in mathematics. These indices usually possess integer values. This habit is also re-
flected in the programming language Fortran in that all variable names which start with the letters

        I,J,K,L,M or N

automatically possess the type INTEGER unless the particular
names have not been explicitly declared. Variable names which
start with the letters different from I,J,K,L,M,N are automatically assigned the type REAL unless they have been explicitly
declared.

---

[*] One should be aware that the definition of the constant names
is static for every compilation. It is not possible to have a
dynamic organization of the field limits capable of being defined at the time of execution of the program in Fortran 77.

Apart from the predefined fixing of the type which has just
been illustrated and the earlier described explicit declaration
(with the aid of key words DOUBLE PRECISION, INTEGER, LOGICAL
and REAL which we have considered up to now), there is a
further possibility for implicit definition of the type. It is
controlled by means of the first letter.

For example, if it is desired to define

- all variables whose names begin with A,...,F or M
  so that they possess the type INTEGER,
- all variables whose names begin with L or P
  so that they possess the type LOGICAL,
- and all variables whose names begin with X,Y,Z
  so that they are of REAL,

then this can be achieved by means of the declaration:

IMPLICIT INTEGER (A-F,M), LOGICAL (L,P), REAL (X-Z)

The IMPLICIT declaration has the following general form:

$$\text{IMPLICIT type}_1(\text{area}_1[,\text{area}_2]\ldots)[,\text{type}_2(\text{area}_1[,\text{area}_2]\ldots)]\ldots$$

Type stands for one of the key words of the type definition,
area stands for a range of letters (written with the minus sign)
or for a single letter. A number of different areas can follow
each other, as shown in the example above, but they have to be
separated by commas. This also applies for additional type
definitions.

The following sequence is given in Fortran in order to define
the type of a variable:

1) Explicit declaration
2) IMPLICIT-declaration
3) Predefined definition of the type.

Hence, although an explicit declaration is not necessary for
variables having the type INTEGER and REAL we shall nevertheless declare all variables at the beginning of the program:
It is advisable to declare all items needed in the program at
the beginning of the program. Furthermore, as we have already
seen it is necessary to make the declaration for the case of
fields (vectors, matrices). There is, however, a second
possibility, namely, the use of the DIMENSION statement.

After the key word

    DIMENSION

the name of the field is declared as well as the limits for
the required indices which are placed in parentheses. The type
of the components of the field results from either an explicit
declaration, an IMPLICIT declaration or a predefined type
definition.

Thus, instead of the two statements

```
REAL S(100),X1(0:10,20)
INTEGER N5(-3:60)
```

it is possible to write (predefined type definition):

```
DIMENSION S(100),X1(0:10,20),N5(-3:60)
```
or for the case of explicit type definition:

```
REAL S,X1
INTEGER N5
DIMENSION S(100),X1(0:10,20),N5(-3:60)
```

We shall, however, use the explicit declaration including the
declaration of the limits as, in our opinion, the DIMENSION
declaration makes the program difficult to follow.

At this stage we wish to indicate error possibilities which may
occur in connection with the predefined type definition: If an
error is made when keying in a variable name, then this mistake
cannot be recognized by the compiler. The program is then executed with undefined values for the new variables which have
been created by mistake. The source of error described above
can be minimized by means of the misuse of the IMPLICIT declaration by making the following declaration at the beginning of
the program.

    IMPLICIT LOGICAL (A-Z)

The above statement results in all names, not explicitly declared, being provided with the type LOGICAL and hence cause
an error in the compilation of an arithmetic expression.

The following exercises have been designed to make the user become more acquainted with the use of matrices. The solutions are not necessary for an understanding of the programming language Fortran.

Find the solution vector $X = \begin{pmatrix} x_1 \\ .. \\ x_n \end{pmatrix}$ corresponding to an unequivocal solution of a given system of linear equations

$$a_{11}x_1 + a_{12}x_2 + \ldots + a_{1n}x_n = b_1$$
$$\vdots \qquad\qquad\qquad\qquad \vdots$$
$$a_{n1}x_1 + a_{n2}x_2 + \ldots + a_{nn}x_n = b_n$$

represented by $AX = B$.

Using the Gaussian elimination method, the rows of the system of equations can be transformed into the following form by means of appropriate linear combinations.

$$a'_{11}x_1 + a'_{12}x_2 + \quad \ldots \quad + a'_{1n}x_n = b'_1$$
$$a'_{22}x_2 + \quad \ldots \quad + a'_{2n}x_n = b'_2$$
$$\ddots \qquad\qquad \ldots$$
$$a'_{nn}x_n = b'_n$$

Once the system of equations has been reduced to this triangular form containing the diagonal elements $a'_{kk} \neq 0$ then the components $x_{n-1}, \ldots, x_1$ of the solution vector X can be calculated by starting from x_n. If the diagonal element a'_{kk} and all succeeding elements a'_{jk} (for j greater than k) are zero in one particular column, then the system of equations cannot be solved. The calculation can be discontinued. If, however, an element below the diagonal is not equal to 0, then by means of interchanging the rows, this can then become the diagonal element. The solution vector X is not affected by the interchanging of the rows. In order to keep the rounding errors as small as possible, the interchanging of the rows is always carried out when an element a'_{jk} below the diagonal has a larger absolute value than the element a'_{kk} in the diagonal. (This is called "Pivoting").

<u>Exercise 4.1</u>

Using the Gaussian elimination method determine the solution $x_1, \ldots, x_3$ of the system of equations

$$x_1 + 0.5x_2 + 0.3x_3 = 1$$
$$0.2x_1 + 2x_2 + 0.4x_3 = 2$$
$$0.2x_1 + 0.2x_2 + x_3 = 3$$

<u>Hint:</u> The above system of equations does not require the interchanging of the rows in order to obtain the solution.

At the end of chapter 3, it was shown, by means of an example, how an iterative method can be used in order to determine the zero positions of the function. An iterative method for the solution of linear equation systems will now be described.

The equation system AX = B can be transformed to give:

$$a_{11}x_1 = \qquad {}^-a_{12}x_2\ {}^-a_{13}x_3\ {}^-\ldots\ {}^-a_{1n-1}x_{n-1}\ {}^-a_{1n}x_n + b_1$$
$$a_{22}x_2 = {}^-a_{21}x_1 \qquad {}^-a_{23}x_3\ {}^-\ldots\ {}^-a_{2n-1}x_{n-1}\ {}^-a_{2n}x_n + b_2$$
$$\vdots \qquad\qquad\qquad\qquad\qquad\qquad\qquad\qquad\qquad \vdots$$
$$a_{nn}x_n = {}^-a_{n1}x_1\ {}^-a_{n2}x_2\ {}^-a_{n3}x_3\ {}^-\ldots\ {}^-a_{nn-1}x_{n-1} \qquad + b_n$$

Since it can be assumed that – if necessary after interchanging the rows – the elements a_{jj} are not equal to zero, a new equation system can be obtained having the form

$$X = C \cdot X + D$$

The following obviously applies for the elements of the matrix C

$$c_{jk} = \begin{cases} -\dfrac{a_{jk}}{a_{jj}} & \text{for } k = 1, \ldots, n \text{ with } k \neq j \\[2ex] 0 & \text{for } k = j \end{cases}$$

and for the components of the vector D

$$d_j = \frac{b_j}{a_{jj}} \qquad \text{for } j = 1, \ldots, n$$

An iteration can be derived from the new system of equations:

$$X^{(m+1)} = X^{(m)}C + D \qquad \text{for } m = 0, 1, \ldots$$

or explicitly

$$x_j^{(m+1)} = \sum_{k=1}^{n} c_{jk} x_k^{(m)} + d_j \qquad \text{for } j = 1, \ldots, n$$

Thus, starting from the initial vector $X^{(0)}$ successive approximation vectors $X^{(m)}$ can be calculated in the hope that they will converge to the solution vector X of the initial system of equations.

When programming, however, the iterative method just described has the disadvantage that the vector $X^{(m)}$ has to be available until the last component of the approximation vector $X^{(m+1)}$ has been calculated for every iterative step (thus the name "Gesamtschrittverfahren" which means total-step method). As a result two completely different vectors are necessary for $X^{(m)}$ and $X^{(m+1)}$ and not simply one vector as is the case for the so-called "Einzelschrittverfahren" or single-step method. In the single-step method, the components of the vector $X^{(m+1)}$ which have already been calculated are used instead of the components of $X^{(m)}$ for the calculation of the remaining components of $X^{(m+1)}$. The components $x_j^{(m+1)}$ can be expressed in a formula as follows:

$$x_j^{(m+1)} = \sum_{k=1}^{j-1} c_{jk} x_k^{(m+1)} + \sum_{k=j+1}^{n} c_{jk} x_k^{(m)} + d_j$$

for $j = 1, \ldots, n$

Exercise 4.2

Using the single-step method solve the equation system given in Exercise 4.1.

Hint: 1) The convergence conditions are fulfilled.

2) The iteration can be discontinued when the component of two successive approximation vectors differ by less then 10^{-4}.

5 Output on the Printer or the Terminal

In the programs we have considered up to now a standard format was used for the output of variable values and it was unimportant where and in which manner the variables were printed. Furthermore, we have purposely neglected to describe how to output titles etc. and the possibility to output data in an orderly manner.

This possibility will now be discussed in detail starting with the output using standard output devices, i.e. the printer or the terminal. Finally, we will be able to see the similarities with the input of data.

The following general form can be used for the output of data.

WRITE (*,f) output list

f FORMAT $\left(\begin{array}{l}\text{details of the type and the print position of the}\\\text{variables to be output}\end{array}\right)$

The asterisk (*) in the first parentheses after the key word WRITE indicates that the output of the values should be accomplished by means of the standard output device. The output can be transferred to other devices - such as, for example, magnetic tape units or magnetic disk units - by means of different numbers. This will, however, be considered in detail later.

The number f which follows the comma links, in an unequivocal manner, the WRITE statement with a FORMAT statement which possesses f as a statement number. Hence the FORMAT statement can be placed anywhere in the program, i.e. it is not necessary for it to directly follow the WRITE statement. Furthermore, the same FORMAT can be used for different WRITE statements.

The output list contains all names of storage places whose contents are to be output by means of a WRITE statement. The names are separated by commas. This may be used for the output of simple variables and individual components of vectors or elements of matrices as well as for constants, arithmetic or logical expressions. [*] After the description of the FORMAT statement it will be shown how vectors and matrices can be output.

____

[*] It is not allowed to output constants or expressions in the subset.

The display has 80 and the printer 133 positions per line which
are available for output.[*] The first position of each line
output on the printer is used for controlling the paper feed.
(This will be explained later). There are, therefore, 132
printing positions per line which can be used by the FORMAT
statement. These 132 positions can be used for the output of
letters and special characters. The following format codes are
provided for the output of numbers:

     I   for numbers of type INTEGER
     E or F for numbers of type REAL
     D or F for numbers of type DOUBLE PRECISION

The format code L is provided for items having the type
LOGICAL.

The format code

     Z

can be used on some computers for the output of the contents
of the storage place of any particular type. This does not,
however, belong to the standard version of Fortran 77.

The format codes are linked to the "field width" w, i.e. the
total number of printing positions provided for the number
to be output. Moreover, for the output of numbers having the
type REAL or DOUBLE PRECISION, the number d, denoting the
number of digits behind the decimal point, has to be given.
Finally, r ("repetition factor") represents more than one format code having the same form. The individual items of the information are assigned to the format codes in the following
forms:

     rIw
     rEw.d   or   rFw.d
     rDw.d   or   rFw.d
     rLw
and   rZw | not included in standard Fortran 77

---

[*] a) For reasons of simplification, we shall limit ourselves to a
    description of the printer output in the following. The out-
    put on the terminal is very similar.
  b) Some printers even provide for 136 print positions per line;
    however, on small systems (e.g. personal computers) very
    often only 80 positions are allowed.

If the number r is not given, then it is taken as 1. For example, the following format[*]

    1OO FORMAT (1X,2I4)

enables the output of 2 numbers of the type INTEGER, each being allowed to possess not more than 4 digits. If a number is negative, then in order to obtain the correct output, the above format is allowed to have a maximum of 3 digits since one print position is required for the negative sign. If the output field for a number to be output is too small due to incorrect choice of the constant w, then the output field is filled with a series of asterisks.

If it is required to output numbers having the type REAL or DOUBLE PRECISION using the format codes E and D, then the numbers are printed in a normalized form. Due to the normalization and the sign, the field width w must be at least 7 print positions greater than the number d of the digits which are to be printed behind the decimal point.[**]

$$(\pm)0.\underbrace{\ldots\quad\ldots}_{d\ \text{digits}}E(\pm)ee \qquad \text{or} \qquad (\pm)0.\underbrace{\ldots\quad\ldots}_{d\ \text{digits}}D(\pm)ee$$

Thus, for example, the output of the number -23.61 requires a field width w of at least 11 if the E format code is to be used, i.e. the code must be

    E11.4

if all digits are to be printed. The number which is output has the following form

    $-0.2361E+02$ $(= -0.2361 \cdot 10^{2})$

If the field width w chosen is greater than 11 (in general: greater than (d+7)), then blanks are included to the left of the number in the field declared. If the chosen field width w is too small, then the field provided for the number is filled with a series of asterisks.

---

[*] The meaning of 1X will be explained later; it is connected with the vertical feed control of the paper for the printer.

[**] In some compilers, the digit 0 in front of the decimal point is omitted and as a result the field width w must only be greater than d by at least 6 printing positions.

If a number having the type REAL or DOUBLE PRECISION is to be printed with a fixed decimal point, then the F code should be used. This also requires that the chosen field width w is large enough for the field to accept all digits, the decimal point and, if necessary, a negative sign. Please note, any zeros included behind the decimal point, have to be counted too. For example, the code F6.2 can be used for the output of -23.61. The output provided by the printer would be -23.61. However if it is desired to print 3 numbers after the decimal point, then the format F7.3 has to be used. This results in the number -23.610 being printed. If the field width w in the example has been chosen to be greater than 6 or 7, then the field comprises of blanks placed before the number. On the other hand, however, if the field width w had been chosen to be too small, then the output field would have been filled with asterisks.

If a FORMAT statement comprises of a number of format codes and if the output list of corresponding WRITE statements consists of several variable names, then

> the first variable is assigned to the first format code, the second variable is assigned to the second format code etc.

Example 5.1

```
      REAL X,Y
      INTEGER K,N
      N = 31
      K = 208
      X = -0.043
      Y = 7.1
      WRITE (*,103) N,X,Y,K
  103 FORMAT (1X,I3,2E11.3,I2)
      . . .
```

In the above example

> N   is printed according to the code I3
>
> X   is printed according to the code E11.3
>
> Y   is printed according to the code E11.3
>
> K   is printed according to the code I2

The line which is printed on pager is illustrated on the next page:

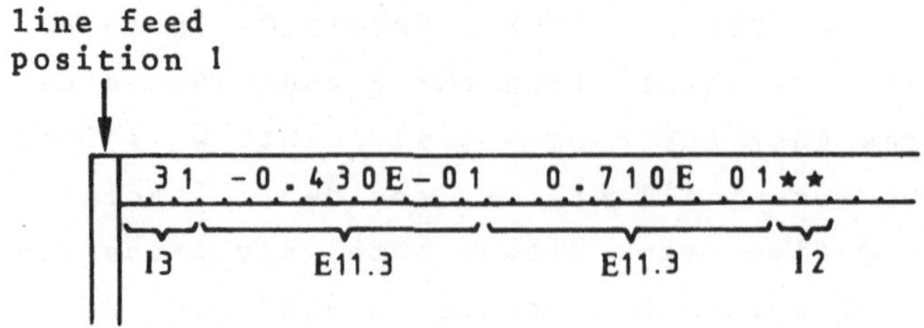

Two asterisks can be seen in the last output field which is described by means of the format code I2 to provide for the output of the variable K. This is the result of K possessing the value 208, i.e. more than 2 digits.

Now it is quite possible that the user does not wish various numbers to be printed so close to one another; instead it is required that the numbers should be separated by blanks. This type of output can be achieved quite simply by increasing the field width w of the various format codes. For example, if the above format having the number 103 was changed as follows

    103 FORMAT (1X,I6,2E13.3,I5)

then the above WRITE statement would result in the following printed line:

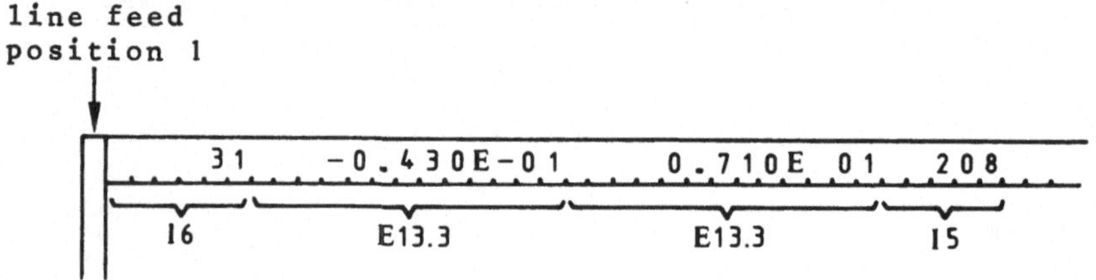

There is a further possibility to separate two successive fields by means of blanks, namely, by applying an additional format code. The declaration

    rX

results in r blanks being left between neighbouring fields. For example, if the WRITE statement used in Example 5.1 calls the following format

    103 FORMAT (1X,I3,2X,E11.3,2X,E11.3,3X,I2)

then the following line will be printed:

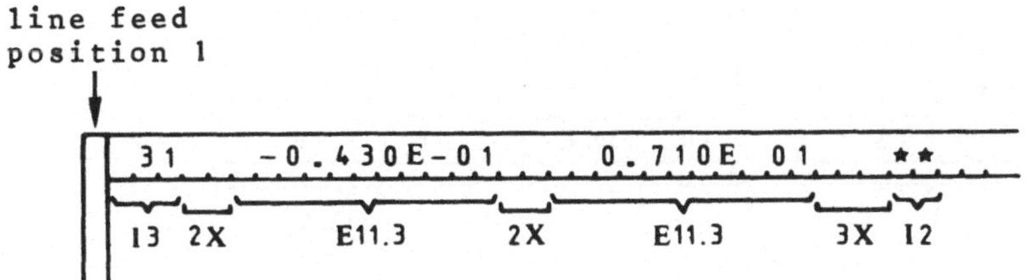

(Please note the different output of K).

It is possible to combine not only the same format codes, but also sequences of format codes. They can be placed in parentheses and the number of times they are to be repeated is declared before the parentheses. Hence,

    103 FORMAT (1X,I3,2(2X,E11.3),3X,I2)

results in the same output line as above.

The tabulator can be used as an additional possibility to separate a series of output fields. It has the code

    Tp | not included
                                          | in the subset

and results in the printing of all fields listed after Tp in the format from the printing position p onwards. For example, the format

    103 FORMAT (1X,I3,T7,E11.3,T20,E11.3,T31,I5)

in conjunction with the WRITE statement of Example 5.1, results in the line

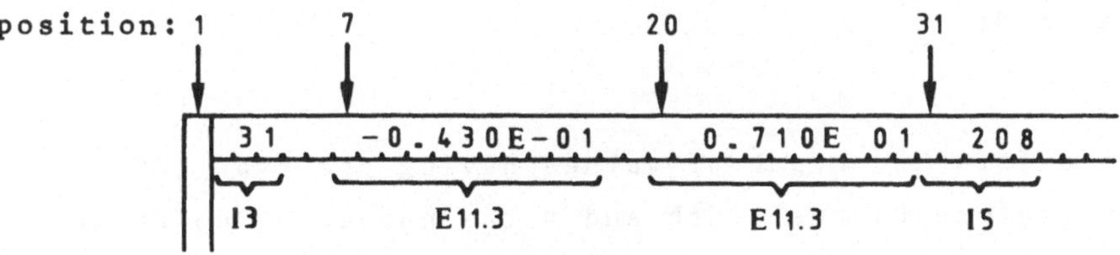

The tabulator code which follows at a later point is, of course, allowed to have a smaller value of p than its predecessor, i.e. the tabulator can be moved backwards. Thus

        WRITE (*,103) N,X,Y,K
    103 FORMAT (1X,I3,T15,2E11.3,T5,I5)

using the values for N,X,Y,K in Example 5.1 the following line is obtained:

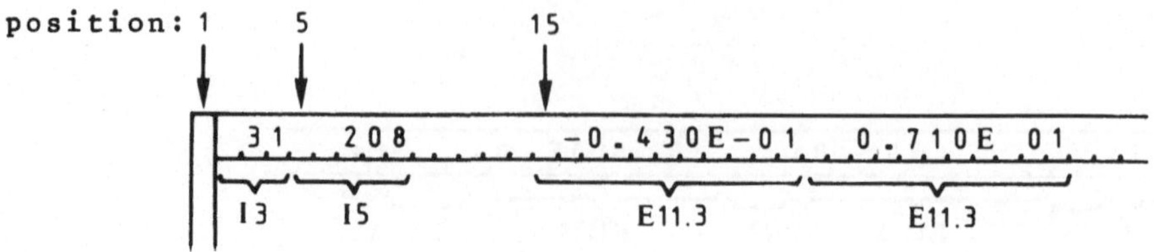

In addition to the tabulator code Tp which for all intents
and purposes fixes the "absolute" position in the output line,
Fortran 77 (i.e. the full version) provides for two codes
which are capable of moving the tabulator relative to the
current value. These are

    TRr   which moves the tabulator "r" positions to the
            right
and TLr   which moves it "r" positions to the left.

It is obvious that the code

    TRr   is identical to the declaration rX
            illustrated on page 42.

As described above, the assignment of the variables required
for output to the various format codes depends only on the
sequence of the variables in the WRITE statement. Over and
above this, the sequence of the values to be output in a
particular print line, depends on the "absolute" or "relative"
tabulator declarations.[*)]

The format code

    rLw

is provided for the output of values having the type LOGICAL,
whereby w represents the width and r the number of codes which
are the same. If the variable has the value

    .TRUE.

then the letter T is printed after w-1 blanks. If the value is

    .FALSE.

then the letter F will be printed instead of T.

[*)] Backward positioning of the tabulator should be avoided, since
it usually leads to confusion.

As already mentioned on page 39 the format code

    rZw

does not belong to the standard version of Fortran 77. However, since this code is often required and accepted by many compilers, we shall describe its function here.

The Z code serves to output the contents of a storage place in hexadecimal form and it is irrelevant what kind of type the variable possesses which belongs to the storage place. A hexadecimal digit comprises of 4 bits and in order to output the contents of a 32 bit word we have to declare the code Z8.

We shall now illustrate how titles and intermediate texts can be output. This is carried out by placing the required text in apostrophes in the format corresponding to the WRITE statement. For example, the following statements

```
      WRITE (*,104)
  104 FORMAT(1X,'RESULTS')
```

result in the following line being printed:

line feed
position 1

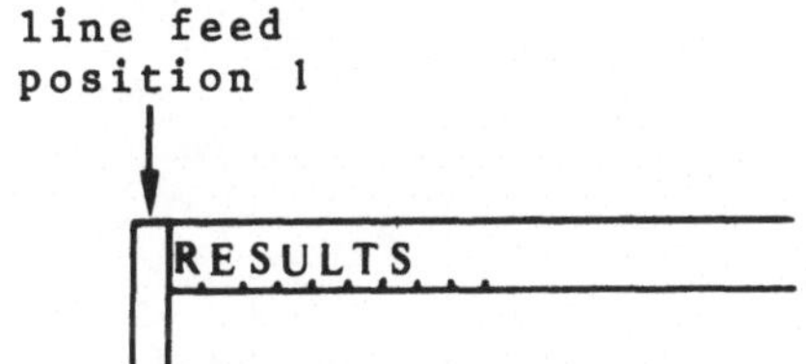

It is also possible to combine the output of texts and variable values. Thus, using the values from Example 5.1 and the follo-wing statements

```
      WRITE (*,103) N,X,Y,K
  103 FORMAT (1X,' NO =',I3,' X =',E11.3,3X,
     *'Y =',F4.2,' K  =',I4)
```
                                                continuation
                                                line (cf. page 7)

the following printed line is obtained:

line feed
position 1

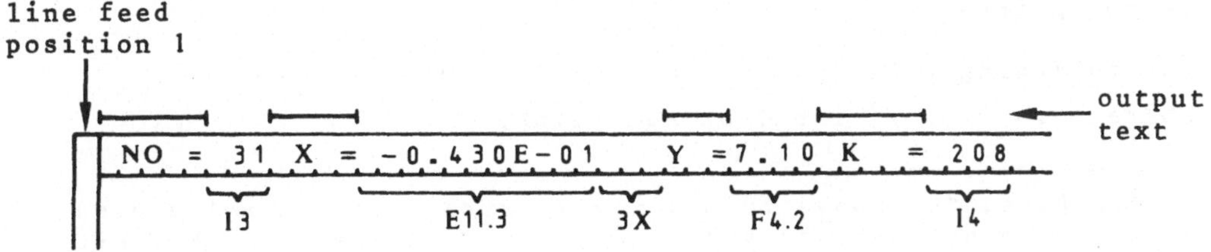

If an apostrophe is required in the output text, then at the appropriate position in the format, two apostrophes directly following one another have to be declared, from which one will be used in the output.

As an alternative to the output form for texts which has just been described, texts can also be defined by means of the following format code.[*)]

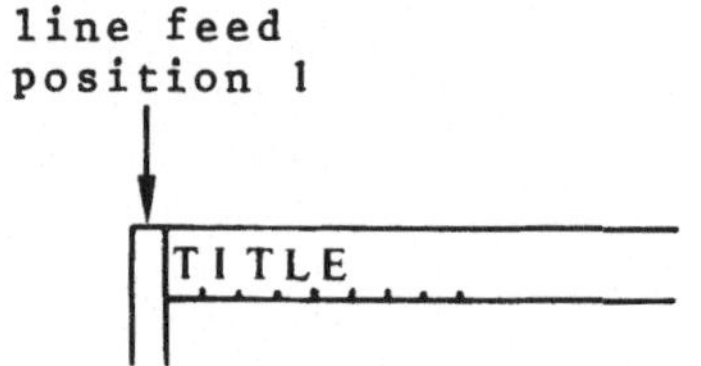

When using the H code (from "Hollerith") it is only necessary to use one character for the output of an apostrophe. Thus

```
      WRITE (*,102)
  102 FORMAT (1X,5HTITLE)
```

results in the following line being printed:

The most important format codes which are necessary to obtain an output line in a clearly arranged manner have already been explained. It is now necessary to describe the tools required to print a line on a page in an optimal manner.

As already mentioned above, position 1 of each line serves, with the aid of certain control characters, to inform the printer how much paper has to be advanced before the rest of the lines (positions 2 up to 133) can be printed. The character required for control the line feed ("vertical control character") is not printed.

The following table shows the effect of placing certain characters in position 1 of each line:

[*)] In practice, the above form using apostrophes is usually used, since it is not necessary to count the characters in the text.

blank	one line feed	printing is done in the next line
digit 0	two line feeds	one blank line
+	no line feed	printing is done in the same line
digit 1	skip to the next page	printing is done in the first line of the next page
other characters	depends on the computer in use	

It should be noted that it makes no difference how these characters are assigned to the "print position" 1: The character placed in position 1 is interpreted as a vertical control character and is not printed.

For example, if the INTEGER number N has the value 148, then

```
      WRITE (*,104) N
  104 FORMAT (I3)
```

results in the sequence of digits 48 being printed on the next page.

line feed
position 1

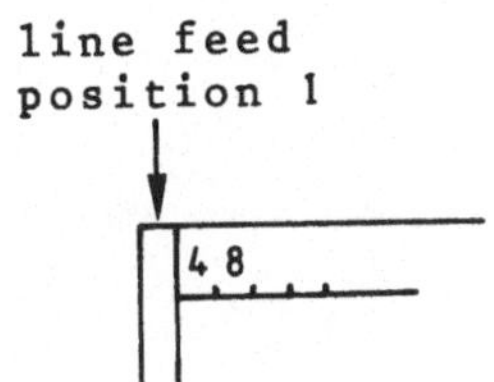

Up to now the code 1X has been at the beginning of every output format for placing a blank in position 1. It has the effect that the output is advanced by one line. The same effect can be achieved by means of the following FORMAT statements

```
n₁  FORMAT(T2,...)        | full Fortran only
n₂  FORMAT('␣',...)
n₃  FORMAT(1H␣,...)
```

The three dots in the above FORMAT refer to the format codes. The second and third possibility show how the other vertical control characters can be placed in position 1: The required control characters are either included in the first format code between the two apostrophes or after the 1H. For example,

```
      WRITE (*,100)
  100 FORMAT ('1','TITLE')
or
  100 FORMAT (1H1,'TITLE')
```

enables the text TITLE to be printed in the first line of the
next page. The same can be achieved by the following formats

```
  100 FORMAT ('1TITLE')
or
  100 FORMAT (6H1TITLE)
```

The slash / (division sign) provides a further possibility
for the control of the output by the printer. It is used within a format and indicates that a new line (with a new vertical
control character) has to be printed and that it includes the
contents following the slash. For example,

```
      WRITE (*,105) N,X,Y,K
  105 FORMAT ('1 N =',I3/2E10.2/'0 K =',I3)
```

enables the values in Example 5.1 (page 41) to be printed on
a new page:

line feed
position 1

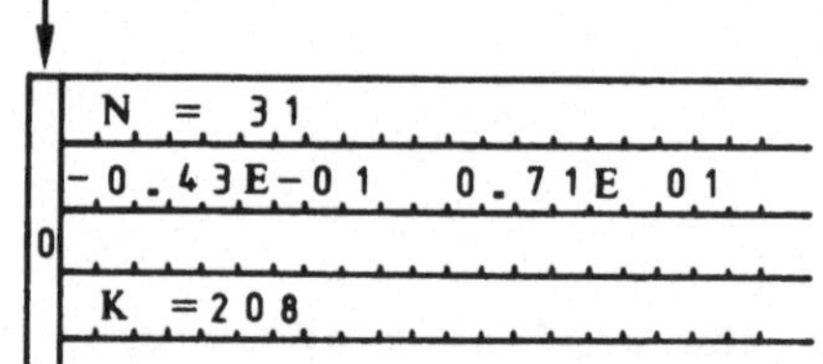

If n slashes directly follow each other, then (n-1) blank
lines will be printed.

If the list of the variable names in the WRITE statement is
greater than that specified in the output code of the format,
then the remaining variables are printed in the following
manner:

1)   The line being considered is printed and a new one started.

2)a) The computer notes, within a format specification (i.e.
     within the parentheses), the last pair of parentheses.
     This parentheses field which includes repetition factors
     etc. as far as the end of the format declaration, is used

as the format specification for the remaining variables
(if necessary, more than once, whereby a new line is
started each time). Care has to be taken that corresponding
output codes are available which fit the variables.

 b) If no further pairs of parentheses exist within the format
    specification, then the whole format is used once again.
    (If necessary, more than once, whereby a new line is
    started each time).

<u>Example:</u>

   Slashes are not required in the following format declarations:
       WRITE (*,100) list of variables

a)   100 FORMAT (..(..)..(..)..)
                                       format codes for the 1st line
                                       format codes for the 2nd line
                                       and the following lines

b)   100 FORMAT (..2(..(..)..)..)
                                       format codes for the 1st line
                                       format codes for the 2nd line
                                       and the following ones

c)   100 FORMAT (...)
                                       format codes for all the lines

<u>Exercise 5.1</u>

   It is required to know how strongly 2 variables, both
   having only two possibilities, are related to one another.
   An application of the so-called four-field correlation
   method can supply certain results. (As an example the
   question will be posed: Do boys or girls prefer sport?)
   The following table can be compiled:

	+	-
B	a	b
G	c	d

a: number of boys who like sport
b: number of boys who do not like sport
c: number of girls who like sport
d: number of girls who do not like sport

   The above table can be extended by means of summing
   respective rows and columns. This results in

	+	−	
B	a	b	a+b
G	c	d	c+d
	a+c	b+d	a+b+c+d

The following numbers are supplied

$$a = 28 \quad b = 61 \quad c = 19 \quad d = 72$$

Using these values, print the modified table with vertical and horizontal lines.

<u>Hint:</u> A horizontal line can be simulated by means of a sequence
of minus signs. Instead of using the format code

```
'--------'
```

it is easier to simply write 8('-').

A vertical line can be produced by means of the letter I
being printed one under the other.

In the examples up to now which have been used to illustrate
output statements, only simple variables have been used in the
variable list. It will now be shown how values of vectors and
matrices can be printed.

Since every vector component and every matrix element is
comprised of simple variables, the individual elements of a
field can be accessed using what we already know. Over and
above this, there is the possibility to simply declare the
name of the vector or matrix in the list of the WRITE statement. This results in the complete field being printed in the
same sequence as that which is internally stored in columns
(cf. page 31). The manner in which the individual values are
printed depends, however, on the format code used.

The so-called "implicit DO-loop" can be used as a possibility
for the output of fields (if necessary also parts of fields).
It has the general form:

```
(list, d = a, e, i)
```

where 'list' represents one or more items separated by commas.
As was mentioned at the beginning of this chapter, these items
can be:

- name of a variable
- vector component or matrix element
- name of a vector or a matrix
- expressions

The items: DO-variable d, initial value a, final value e and
the increment i, have exactly the same meaning as those
described on page 24 of the DO statement. The declared values
of the 'list' are printed for d = a, a+i, a+2i, ... according
to the format code. Since the 'list' can contain an implied
DO-loop, it is obvious that several loops can be nested within one another.

<u>Exercise 5.2</u>

The matrix A is declared by

    REAL A(3,2)

and its elements A(j,k) are assigned the values
j + k/10.0. How are the values printed in the output
format if

    100 FORMAT (2F4.1)

is used and the following output statements are made?

a)   WRITE (*,100) A
b)   DO 1111 J = 1,3,1
        WRITE (*,100) (A(J,K), K=1,2,1)
   1111 CONTINUE
c)   WRITE (*,100) ((A(J,K), K=1,2,1), J=1,3,1)

6 The Input of Data

In this chapter it will be shown how to input data by means of
the 'standard input unit'. This is either the input console
('keyboard') for interactive program execution or an assigned
file for the case of program execution in batch operation.

Every data line is comprised of 80 input positions which are
read by means of an input statement (READ) and interpreted
by means of a corresponding format statement. The general input
form is as follows:[*)]

  READ (*,f) input list

  f FORMAT $\left(\begin{array}{l}\text{details regarding position and information}\\ \text{about how the variables receive their values}\end{array}\right)$

Only the names of (simple) variables, vectors and matrices as
well as their components are allowed to be used in the input
list. It is not allowed to use constants, arithmetic or logical
expressions. With this exception, the input list has the same
structure as the output list in the WRITE statement.

The individual input fields are described by format codes in
exactly the same manner as was the case for the output:

rIw		for INTEGER	
rEw.d	rFw.d	for REAL	
rDw.d	rFw.d	for DOUBLE PRECISION	not in subset
rLw		for LOGICAL	

Positions can be skipped by means of

  rX

The tabulator codes

  Tp, TRa, TLa   not in subset

can be used in exactly the same manner as was described for
the output.

The format codes nH... and '...' which enable the output of
texts, are not permitted for the input in Fortran 77.

[*)] The list directed input is especially convenient for interactive programming. It is therefore recommended to use the list
directed input which is, however, only possible in full
Fortran 77 (cf. page 58).

If the input data is written in the input line in the same
manner as it would appear in an output line using the same
format, then the values are transferred correctly to the variables. If this input form is not used, other values can be given
to the variables. These variations will now be described.

The values are not "right aligned" in the input field

If the sequence of digits is not input in a right-aligned
manner in an INTEGER field (code Iw) then zeros are inserted
up to the right hand margin. As a result the input value is
increased by an amount corresponding to many times the power
of 10. For example, the input of

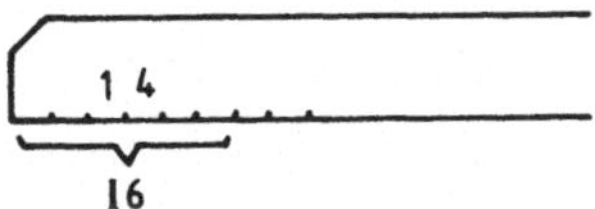

results in the value 1400 being transferred. The same applies
when using the E or D codes by writing the numbers to be input with exponents in the specified field. For example, if
the number $0.78 \cdot 10^3$ is input in a field described by the format code E10.2 and the input form is as follows

then the value $0.78 \cdot 10^{30}$ will be transferred, since the last
position of the field is interpreted as a zero.

Values possessing a decimal point in the input field

If it is desired to input a value having a decimal point and
without an exponent using the format codes Dw.d, Ew.d or
Fw.d, then it is not necessary for the value to be right
aligned: If zeros are added after the decimal point, this does
not change the value. In this case the number of digits d in
the format codes plays no role: The value described in the input field which is used is the one described by the w positions,
no matter if the format codes D, E or F are used. Over and
above this, the condition $w \geqslant d + 7$ for the codes D and E
can be neglected (cf. page 40).

<u>Values not possessing a decimal point</u>

If, for the case of the format codes Dw.d, Ew.d, or Fw.d, the input field contains only a sequence of digits, then a decimal point will be automatically inserted. It is inserted between positions d and (d+1) counting from the right hand of the corresponding input field.[*] For example, the format code F5.2 (also for E5.2 or D5.2)

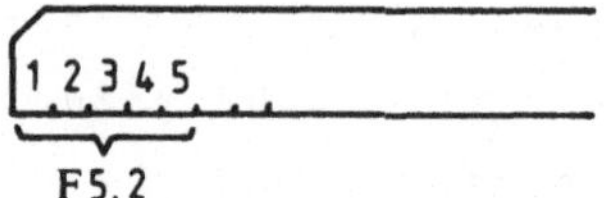

results in the value 123.45 being read.
Similarly

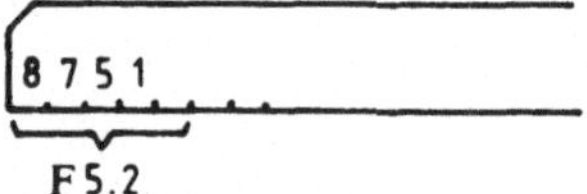

results in the value 875.10 being transferred to the corresponding variable.
It is, however, advisable not to take advantage of this possibility, as it can very easily lead to errors.

It has already been shown that blanks in the input field are interpreted as zeros. This is also true if the blanks occur within a sequence of digits. For example, the format code F5.2 and the following input field

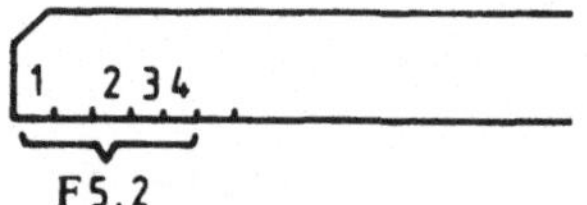

results in the value 102.34 being transferred.

This interpretation of blanks as zeros is given with the declaration BZ in the format statement. Since this is default, it is not necessary to mention it; if it is required to cancel it, then BN has to be placed before the other format codes. This results in all blanks in the input field being neglected and the remaining characters are interpreted as numbers.[**]

---

[*] In the past this provided the possibility to save place on the punch cards.

[**] In general, we advise against the use of BN and BZ.

<u>Example:</u>

```
    READ (*,100) M
100 FORMAT (BN,I6)
```

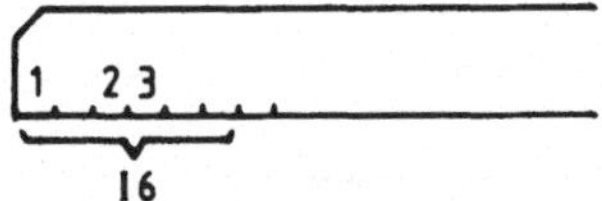

M is given the value 123 since the placing of BN in the format
results in the blanks being ignored.

All vertical control characters necessary for the printer output are, of course, neglected when using the format for input.
If, however, vertical control characters are declared, then
they are interpreted in a different manner. If the vertical
control character was coded as a blank character by means of

```
f FORMAT (1X,...)
```

then the first column of the data line would be ignored. On
the other hand, if vertical control character v is declared
by apostrophes or the format code 1H as follows:

```
f FORMAT (' ',...)
```

or

```
f FORMAT (1H ,...)
```

then this will result in the program being stopped with an
error message when using Fortran 77.

Instead of using the vertical control character as was described
for the printer output, there are two other possibilities to control the transition from one input line to the next by means of a
single READ statement: On the one hand, slashes can be used in
the format declaration, and on the other hand a format code
can be repeated for the case that the input list has not been
completely utilized.

The following examples will illustrate these two possibilities
which can, of course, be combined.

Example 6.1a

```
    READ (*,101) N,X,I2,A1,F4,Z5
101 FORMAT (I3,F5.1,I4/E10.7,F8.3/E10.1)
```

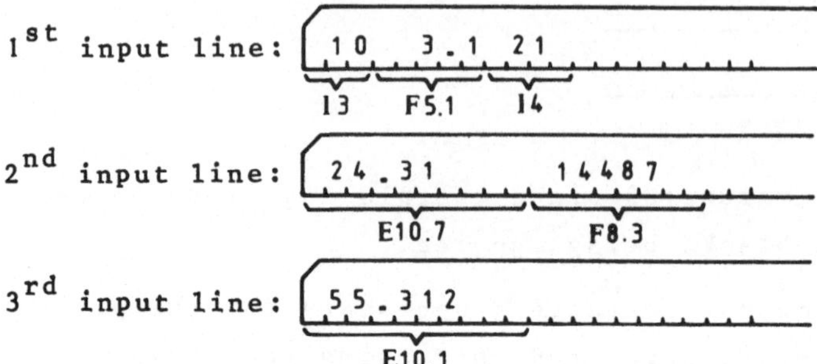

The READ statement results in the variables possessing the
following values:

from the first input line N = 10   X = 3.1   I2 = 210
from the second input line A1 = 24.310000   F4 = 1448.700
from the third input line Z5 = 55.312000

Example 6.1b

```
    READ (*,100) N,X,Y,Z
100 FORMAT (I3,(T4,F7.2))
```

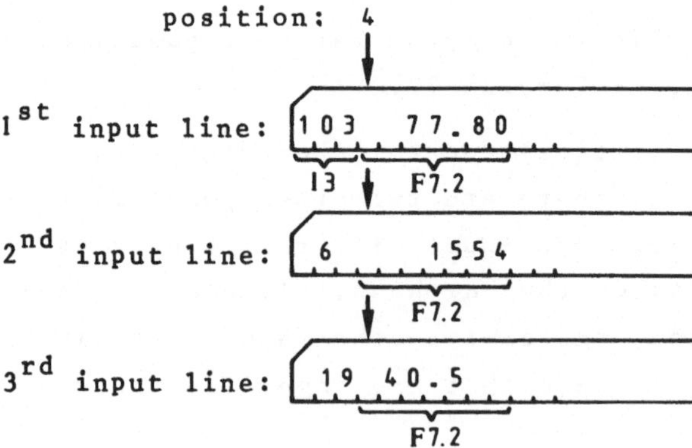

The above results in the following values being transferred:

from the first input line   N = 103   X = 77.80
from the second input line   Y = 15.54
from the third input line   Z = 40.500

The values 6 and 19 in the second and third input lines are ignored because of the tabulator code T4. (Use of the tabulator is not possible in the subset, instead: 3X).

The possibility shown in Example 6.1b is especially useful for the input of vectors and matrices.

Exercise 6.1

    a) Which values are transferred as a result of the input lines in the following program section?

```
      INTEGER J,N
      REAL A(0:10)
      READ (*,100) N,(A(J),J=0,N,1)
  100 FORMAT (I2,(T5,2F5.1))

        . . .
```

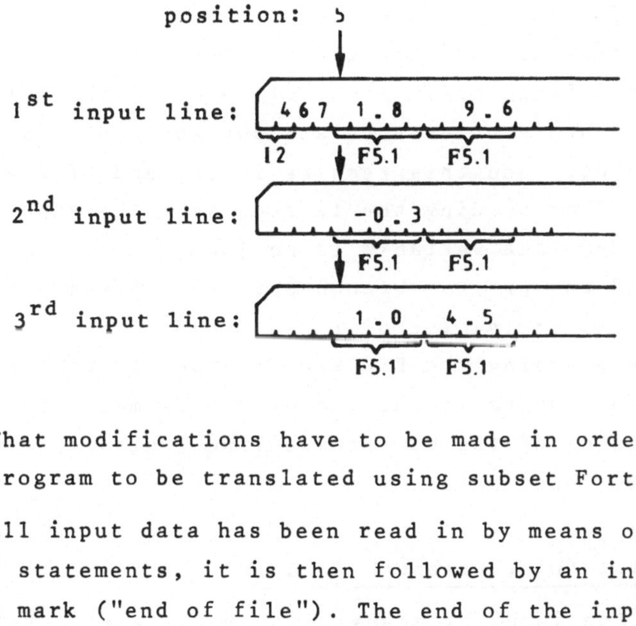

```
              position:  5
                         |
                         v
 1st input line:  | 4 6 7   1 . 8      9 . 6
                    12      F5.1        F5.1

 2nd input line:  |          - 0 . 3
                               F5.1       F5.1

 3rd input line:  |          1 . 0   4 . 5
                             F5.1      F5.1
```

    b) What modifications have to be made in order for the program to be translated using subset Fortran 77?

After all input data has been read in by means of a sequence of READ statements, it is then followed by an input line with the EOF mark ("end of file"). The end of the input file is thus fixed. When carrying out interactive program execution, the EOF mark is usually accomplished by pressing the key ETX or the two keys CNTL and D simultaneously. If, after this, an attempt is made to read new data, then the program stops with an error message. In order to prevent this, a further parameter is provided for in the general form of the READ statement:

```
READ (*,f,END=m)  input list
```

As soon as this form of the "end of file mark" has been read (and interpreted) by means of a READ statement, the input procedure is stopped and the computer branches to the statement having the number m. The program then continues at the m, whereby, of course, all further input of data is impossible. The following exercise can be used to apply this:

Exercise 6.2

If n measurements $x_1, x_2, \ldots, x_n$ are given, write a program to determine the mean value m

$$m = \frac{1}{n} \sum_{i=1}^{n} x_i$$

without having any prior knowledge of the value n of input values.

It is now necessary to indicate the source of error which can take place by the interactive input of data: If the ETX key is pressed immediately after the last character of the last number to be input, then this results in the end of the input being effected after reading the last number. The READ procedure is terminated (the variable is no longer assigned the final value) and the program branches to that statement defined by END = ... It is, therefore, advisable to input "return" before pressing the ETX key in order to complete the input line. This results in the end of a file mark being the first character of the next input line (which does not contain any more input data).

Format Free Input (List Directed Input)

The control of the input by means of formats is especially difficult for the case of (interactive) input using the keyboard. The full version, not however the subset, thus provides for a "list directed input". The format number in the READ statement is replaced by a multiplication sign. It must have a corresponding input with the respective numbers being separated by commas.

<u>Example:</u>

    READ (*,*) N,M,X,Y

<u>Input line:</u>

    4, 106, 7.8,-0.66

The above results in the variables having the following values:

    N = 4 M = 106   X = 7.8 and Y = -0.66

It is useful and also to be recommended to assign a value in
the input line to every variable of the input list; this is,
however, not absolutely necessary. If several commas are
placed one after the other, then the corresponding variables
remain unchanged:

<u>Example:</u>

    READ (*,*) N,M,X,Y

<u>Input line:</u>

    4,106, ,-0.66

The variable X is not assigned a value - the old value is
still valid.
This possibility of retaining the values of variables appears
to be very convenient, however, it should not be overlooked
that it results in creating difficulties when searching for
errors.

7 Internal Representation of Characters, Initialization of Variables

Up to now different characters such as letters, digits and
special signs have been used without going into any details
about how they are represented in the computer. This chapter
is intended to fill this gap as we are of the opinion that it
is often useful to know how the characters are internally represented. The following will apply even if the computer being
used is different to the one described here. Furthermore, it
is assumed that a character (= 1 byte) is encoded by means of
8 bits per unit. The numbers from 0 up to 2^8-1 = 255 can be
presented in the binary system in this unit. If a binary
number between 0 and 255 is used for encoding characters, then
1 byte can be used to code up to 256 different characters.
How this takes place is, of course, arbitrary, but must then
be adhere to. Here we will use the EBCDI code[*)] which has
been defined as follows:

bitposition 4 — 7

bitposition 0 — 3

	0	1	2	3	4	5	6	7	8	9	A	B	C	D	E	F
0																
1																
2																
3																
4	⌴										¢	.	<	(	+	|
5	&										!	$	*	)	;	¬
6	−	/									¦	,	%	_	>	?
7											:	#	@	'	=	"
8		a	b	c	d	e	f	g	h	i						
9		j	k	l	m	n	o	p	q	r						
A			s	t	u	v	w	x	y	z						
B																
C	{	A	B	C	D	E	F	G	H	I						
D	}	J	K	L	M	N	O	P	Q	R						
E	\		S	T	U	V	W	X	Y	Z						
F	0	1	2	3	4	5	6	7	8	9						

[*)] Extended Binary Coded Decimal Interchange Code. The EBCDI code
is frequently used by large computers, whilst the smaller ones
often use the ASCII code which is explained in Appendix E.

The table contains all lower-case letters and characters
which can be found on the keyboard of a terminal. Additional
characters for special purposes can be defined using the free
fields. The first hexadecimal digit of a byte (bit positions
0 to 3) is given by the vertical axis of the table and the
second hexadecimal digit (bit positions 4 to 7) is given by
the horizontal axis. For example, it can be easily shown that
the letter G

has the code | C | 7 | or in binary code | 1 | 1 | 0 | 0 | 0 | 1 | 1 | 1 |

Please note that the encoding of a digit (as a character) is
different to the binary encoding of its number. The digit 6
has the code

     | F | 6 | = | 1 | 1 | 1 | 1 | 0 | 1 | 1 | 0 |

whereas the encoding of the number 6 in an INTEGER variable is
in the hexadecimal form

     | 0 | 0 | 0 | 0 | 0 | 0 | 0 | 6 |

It is now necessary to know how to input the different characters as data in the computer and how the different items can be
obtained in the Fortran program. Fortran 77 provides for a
special data type, namely, CHARACTER.

Constants having the type CHARACTER were already considered
when we dealt with the output on the printer (cf. page 45):

> A CHARACTER constant is a sequence of characters en-
> closed in apostrophes. The length of the constant is
> given by means of the number of its characters.

It is sometimes also called a string. Apostrophes at the beginning and end of the sequence of characters do not belong
to the constant. If an apostrophe is to be included in a sequence of characters, then this is achieved by 2 apostrophes
immediately following each other.

Variables having the type CHARACTER are declared at the beginning of the program in a type declaration. After the key word

     CHARACTER

and the declaration of the length of the variables (declared
by means of *length) the individual names are listed and separated by means of commas. For example, the statement

       CHARACTER*10 A,B,C

declares 3 variables having the names A,B,C in which up to 10
successive characters can be stored respectively. If some of
the variables have a different length to the common length
which was declared, then they can be assigned another length
in the declaration[*]. This takes place after their names using
the same form (*length) as shown in the following example:

       CHARACTER*10 A,A1*15,B,B1*20,C

Here the variables		it is advisable to use the declarations
and	A, B and C have the length 10	CHARACTER*10 A,B,C
	A1 the length 15	CHARACTER*15 A1
	B1 the length 20.	CHARACTER*20 B1

Over and above this, the type CHARACTER can be used to declare
vectors and matrices. The limits for the different indices are
declared in parentheses as in the previously described declarations, i.e. after the names. A length declaration may
follow which then applies for all components of the field.

<u>Example:</u>

       CHARACTER*10 A,Z(0:30)*5,B,X(6,20)*15,C

- The simple variables A,B and C are of length 10.
- 31 components have been declared for Z which are each
  capable of storing 5 characters.
- Matrix X has 120 elements each of length 15.

It will be now shown how a character variable can be assigned
a sequence of characters ("string") in the course of the
program. The first possibility is given by the assignment
statement for CHARACTER variables. The simplest form is

---

[*] The length declaration has to be followed by a constant; an
arithmetic expression is not allowed. The maximum permissible
length depends on the computer being used. If no length is
declared, then it is assumed to be 1, i.e.
    CHARACTER and CHARACTER*1
are equivalent.

```
        v = e
```

where

    v   is a simple variable, a component of a vector or an element of a matrix having the type CHARACTER,

    e   is a CHARACTER expression which for the time being means a constant or a variable having the type CHARACTER.

The assignment results in the following:

Starting at the left hand side, the receiving field (v) is filled with the characters of the CHARACTER expression e. If the receiving field is too small, then the remaining characters are omitted (without an error message); if the receiving field is too large, then the remaining places to the right are filled with blanks (40_{hex}). The assignments

```
        A = 'ASSIGNMENTS'
        B = 'FORTRAN'
```

for the variables A and B of the above example result in the following contents:

A `| A S S I G N M E N T |`

B `| F O R T R A N       |`

So-called CHARACTER substrings can be specified for the subfield of a CHARACTER variable (not included in the subset). Characters can be called from this subfield and also transferred to it. The initial position p_1 and the final position p_2 (counting from the left) are required for the specification of a subfield. These positions are separated by a colon and enclosed in parentheses after the name of the variable v. It is allowed for p_1 and p_2 to be integer expressions. For example, A(3:6) accesses the sequence of characters 'SIGN' of the CHARACTER variable A and

```
        C = B(4:7)
```

results in the sequence of characters 'TRAN' being stored in the variable C.

C `| T R A N             |`

It is, therefore, possible to replace a subfield of a variable
that has already been "occupied" or add to it, as for example

    B(9:10) = '77'

This results in B having the following string of characters:

B $\boxed{\text{F O R T R A N} \quad \text{7 7}}$

It is also possible to create subfields for vector components
and matrix elements: The corresponding element has first to be
defined and then - as described above - followed by the required field. Hence

    X(5,10)(1:3)

results in a definition of a subfield of the matrix element
X(5,10) consisting of the first 3 characters (positions 1 to 3).

A concatenation operator (//) is provided for operands having
the type CHARACTER. It serves to combine a sequence of characters c_1 with a sequence of characters c_2

    c_1 // c_2 | not included in the subset

The length of the concatenated sequence of characters is equal
to the sum of the length of both operands and its contents
consist of the characters from c_1 and followed by the characters from c_2. The two operands may be

    - (simple) variables or constants
    - vector components or matrix elements
    - partial concatenates or
    - CHARACTER expressions in parentheses.

For example,

    A = 'TEXT'//'VALUES'

is a permissible concatenation which stores the following
contents in the variable A

A $\boxed{\text{T E X T V A L U E S}}$

The data input provides a further possibility to transfer a
sequence of characters to a CHARACTER variable. This is done -
as already described - by means of a READ statement in conjunction with a FORMAT statement. The following two format
codes[*) are new and are used for the transfer of characters:

     rA   and   rAw

The declaration of the code rA enables that number of characters
to be transferred from the data line which corresponds to the
length of the respective CHARACTER variable of the input list.

If the format code is used in the form rAw, then the field
width w indicates the number of characters to be transferred.
The characters from the input field which are transferred to
the corresponding CHARACTER variable of the input list depend
on the length of the variable. The result is, however, different
to that what would be expected from the above explanation of
the assignment to CHARACTER variables:[**)

If the length l_v of the CHARACTER variable v is larger than
the field width w, then w characters are transferred to the
variable v in a left justified manner and the remaining part
of the field $(l_v - w)$ is filled with blanks.

If the length l_v is smaller than the field width w, then l_v
characters on the right hand side of the field are transferred
to the variable v and the $(w - l_v)$ characters to the left are
omitted.

The format codes rA and rAw are also used for the output of
CHARACTER variables. If the length of the CHARACTER variable
to be output coincides with the field width w, then the codes
rA and rAw are identical and the total contents of the variable v
are output in the field provided for.

If the length l_v of the variable v is greater than the field
width w, then the w characters on the left hand side are out-

---

[*) The letters r and w have the same meaning as in Chapter 6
       r: Repetition factor (= number of same codes),
       w: Field width.

[**) It seems obvious that the reading is interpreted as an assignment of an external character string to an internal variable;
this is, however, incorrect.

put and the (l_v-w) characters <u>to the right</u> of the variable v
are omitted.

If the length l_v is smaller than the field width w, then l_v
characters on the right hand side of the field are output and
blanks <u>inserted to the left</u>.

<u>Exercise 7.1</u>

Which characters are output after processing the following
program segment?

```
      CHARACTER LINE,Z*3,C*4
      LINE = 'HEADLINE'
      WRITE (*,100) 'TITLE: ',LINE
  100 FORMAT (1X, 2A)
      READ (*,101) Z,C
  101 FORMAT (A2,A6)
      WRITE (*,102) Z,C
  102 FORMAT (1X,A6,A2)
      ...
```

input line: XYJKLMNOP

On page 18 of Chapter 3, it was illustrated how arithmetic expressions can be compared with each other. Now a lot of problems require a comparison between characters and sequences of
characters. Furthermore, since every character is coded by an
integer value, the internal comparison between CHARACTER items
is reduced to a comparison between integer values. If the
CHARACTER items consist of more than one character, then characters having the same position are compared with each other. If,
however, both sequences of characters have different length,
then the shorter one is extended with blanks in order to carry
out the comparison.[*)]

<u>Exercise 7.2</u>

Write a program capable of sorting key words. The key
words are declared in the first 20 positions of each data
line and there are no more than 100 key words.

[*)] No other result is obtained other than the truncation of the
longer character string if no character is used in the intermediate field which belongs to the (unoccupied) rows 0 to 3 of
the table on page 60.

As already explained on page 5 of Chapter 1, all variables
have to be assigned a value before they can appear on the right
hand side of an equal sign. However, when it is necessary to
assign initial values to a lot of different variables, vectors
or matrices (cf. for example Exercise 4.1 on page 36), then it
is desirable to have a more compact method of initializing
values. This possibility is provided for by means of the DATA
statement which has to appear after the declaration of the
variables and the fields but before any executable statements
(cf. Appendix D). Initialization of the values takes place
during the translation of the Fortran program and not during
the execution of the program which takes place later. The DATA
statement has the following general form:

DATA list of variables/list of constants/

Every element of the variable list has to be exactly assigned
to a corresponding type declaration in the constant list. The
assignment is carried out in a purely sequential manner.[*]
For example,

DATA A,B,C,D/0,0,0,-7.1/

means that the variables A,...,D are given the following
initial values:

    A = 0
    B = 0
    C = 0
    D = -7.1

Instead of using the above form it is also possible to write:

DATA A,B,C/0,0,0/,D/-7.1/

or DATA A,B,C/3*0/,D/-7.1/

since it is allowed to unite more than one constant (in the
form r*k). A further possibility is given by:

DATA A,B,C,D/3*0,-7.1/

---

[*] The variable and constant lists have to be of the same length
in Fortran 77. Some compilers do allow for different lengths of
the lists without reporting an error and in doing so the surplus
items are ignored.

It is also possible to initialize vectors and matrices, but in doing so it must be taken into account that matrices are stored as vectors (cf. page 31). For example, the declarations

```
INTEGER D(5,4)
DOUBLE PRECISION X(100)
```

followed by the statement

```
DATA X/100*1.DO/,D/5*1,7*0,3,4,6,8,4*2/
```

result in the following initial values:

All 100 components of the vector X contain the value 1.DO and the matrix D has the values

```
1   0   0   8
1   0   0   2
1   0   3   2
1   0   4   2
1   0   6   2
```

It is also allowed to use an implied DO-loop in the variable list in order to define the vector components and matrix elements. This makes the program easy to understand should it be desired to initialize a matrix in a row manner. The above matrix D can thus be initialized by means of the following statement using a sequence of rows:

```
DATA  ((D(J,K),  K = 1,4),  J = 1,5)  | not allowed in the subset
*          /1,0,0,8,
*           1,0,0,2,
*           1,0,3,2,
*           1,0,4,2,
*           1,0,6,2/
```

Initialization of variables having the type CHARACTER takes place analogously to what was said above. It is only necessary to take into account the length that has been defined. If the length 1_v of the variables in the variable list deviates from the constants (1_c) in the constant list, then either

- blanks are inserted to the right of the variable
  (if 1_v is greater than 1_c) or
- characters to the right of the constant are omitted
  (if 1_v is less than 1_c).

Example:

       CHARACTER A,B*4,C(30)*2

       DATA A,B,C / '*', '+-*/', 30*'%' /

       The following initialization is carried out:
       Variable A having the length 1 is given the character *
       Variable B of length 4 is given the characters +-*/
       Vector C having 30 components of length 2 is given the
       characters % (a blank is included to the right, since
       the constant consists of only 1 character).

The following example serves to illustrate the application.

Example 7.1

       It is required to output the function

       $y = 16x^5 - 20x^3 + 5x$ (Chebyshev polynomial of degree 5)
       graphically on the printer for the interval $[-1, 1]$ and
       a step length of 0.05.

The x axis is arranged vertically on the output line, i.e.
parallel to the left side of the paper, in order to obtain a
high degree of flexibility with respect to the size of the interval on the x axis (i.e. for application to other examples).
The (constant) increase of the x values corresponds then to a
line feed. Not only a graphical representation of the function
but also the values of x and y will be output.

The following graph has 51 different printing positions and
these are related to the respective y values:

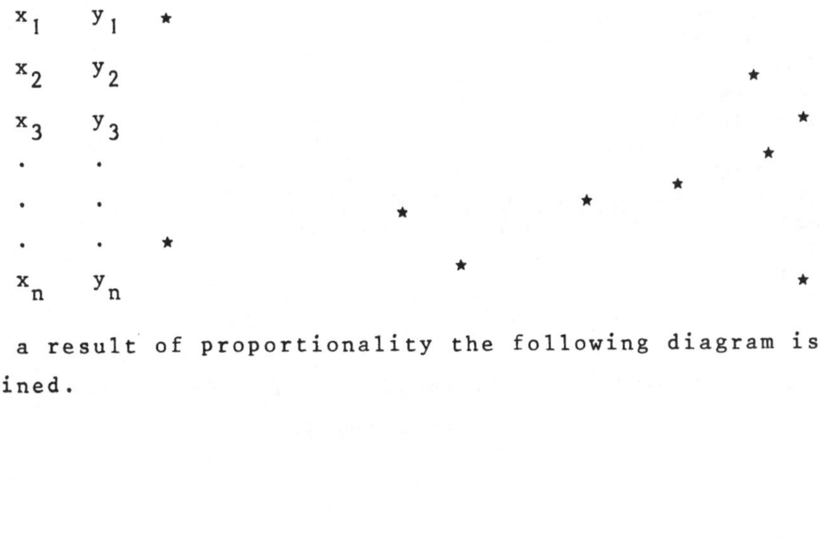

x_1 y_1 *

x_2 y_2 *

x_3 y_3 *

 .   .   *

 .   .   *

 .   .   *

 .   .   *   *

               *   *

x_n y_n *   *

As a result of proportionality the following diagram is obtained.

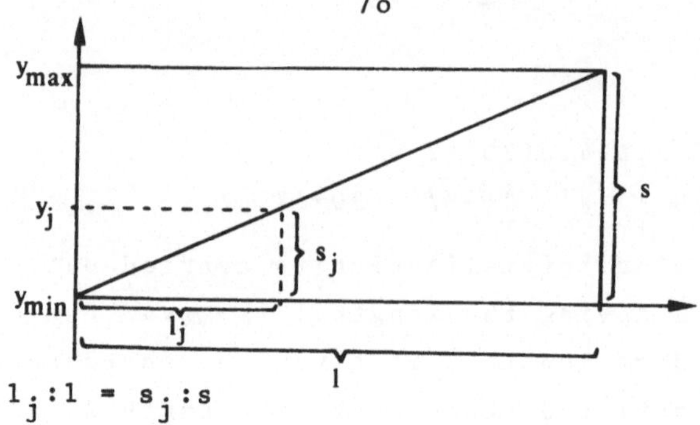

$$l_j : l = s_j : s$$

As we have $\qquad s = y_{max} - y_{min}, \qquad s_j = y_j - y_{min}$

and $\qquad\qquad l = 50$

we get $\qquad\qquad l_j = \dfrac{50}{y_{max} - y_{min}} \cdot (y_j - y_{min})$

The length l_j can thus be given the values $0, 1, \ldots, 50$. Therefore, a vector is necessary in order to output the "curve".
This vector has the type CHARACTER and the indices are from 0
to 50. The values x_j and y_j are stored in the two column vectors
of the matrix VAL (see below). The value 0 can be used for the
initialization of y_{min} and y_{max} since the function y receives
the value 0 in the interval under consideration.

```
      CHARACTER C(0:50),BLANK,ASTER
      REAL X,Y,VAL(100,2),YMIN,YMAX,H
      INTEGER K,L,J,JMAX
      DATA BLANK,C,ASTER /52*' ','*'/,YMIN,YMAX /0.0,0.0/
      JMAX = 0
      DO 1 X = -1,1.01,0.05
      JMAX = JMAX+1
      VAL(JMAX,1) = X
      Y = 16*X**5-20*X**3+5*X
      VAL(JMAX,2) = Y
      IF (Y .GT. YMAX) YMAX = Y
      IF (Y .LT. YMIN) YMIN = Y
    1 CONTINUE
      H = 50/(YMAX-YMIN)
      DO 2 J = 1,JMAX,1
      L = H*(VAL(J,2)-YMIN)
      C(L) = ASTER
      WRITE (*,100) VAL(J,1),VAL(J,2),(C(K), K=0,L,1)
  100 FORMAT (1X,F6.2,F8.3,2X,51A1)
      C(L) = BLANK
    2 CONTINUE
      STOP
      END
```

The programming example is only applicable for full Fortran 77.
Which statements have to be modified for the subset?

8 Subprogram Techniques: Function Subprograms

Using the tools described so far, it is possible, in general, to adequately solve any problem using the language Fortran. Nevertheless, it is necessary to be acquainted with subprogram techniques because of the following reasons:

1) A complicated program can be subdivided into individual subprograms in order for the program to be arranged in an orderly manner. As a result the program can be tested more quickly.

2) Solutions to many common types of problems are already available. These solutions are usually written in the form of a function subprogram or a subroutine.

In this chapter we shall describe the declarations and the calling of function subprograms and in the next chapter the same will be repeated for so-called subroutines. A function subprogram is always exploited when one value (=function value) has to be calculated in dependency of one or more arguments ("parameters") and the same method of calculation would have to be applied at numerous points in the program.

"Formula functions" or "statement functions" represent a simple form of the function subprogram and they are declared by means of a single statement. This type of function has been developed in order to program simple relationships represented by formulas. The declaration of the formula function has the following general form:

    name(lfp) = expression

where

    name   stands for the name of the function,
    lfp   stands for the list of formal parameters,
    expression   stands for an expression of the type
                    CHARACTER, DOUBLE PRECISION, INTEGER,
                    LOGICAL or REAL.[*)]

[*)] Statement functions are only allowed to be of the type INTEGER, LOGICAL or REAL in the subset and consequently only expressions of the same type are permitted.

The declaration has to be made before the first executable statement (cf. Appendix D); it may only be preceded by other declarations. The declared function is then recognized in the program segment up to the statement END.

The type of the formula function has to be defined in a declaration statement by means of specifying the names for the case that it is neither possible nor desirable to refer to the implicitly declared names (cf. page 34). The type of the formula function and the type of the expression on the right side of the assignment sign have to be in accordance with one another or, at least, allow for an assignment.

Formal parameters consist of the names of the simple variables which the formula function depends on. The formal parameters represent storage space reservation (for a particular type) for the actual parameters in the declaration statement which are used when the statement function is called.

Example 8.1

> Example 7.1 (cf. page 69) could have been programmed
> by means of the statement function:
>
> ```
> CHARACTER ...
> REAL ... , X1,FCT
> INTEGER ...                as given in Example 7.1
> DATA ...
> FCT(X1) = 16*X1**5-20*X1**3+5*X1
>
> ...
> ```
>
> The call replaces the arithmetic expressions by means
> of[*)]
>
> $$Y = FCT(X)$$
>
> In doing so, the actual parameter X, having the type REAL,
> replaces the formal parameter X1 in the declaration state-
> ment and the expression is evaluated with the value of X.

[*)] The call of a statement function may also take place in an
(arithmetic) expression depending on the particular problem:
For example,
```
     Y = FCT(X)+3
```
is a permissible call.

It is obvious that the formula function can only be used to describe very simple functional relationships. If the calculation of a function requires a sequence of statements and if the function depends on vectors, matrices or other functions, then the general form of the function subprogram has to be resorted to. Once again we distinguish between

- the declaration and
- the call

of the function subprogram.

The declaration of the subprogram takes place - as opposed to the formula function - outside of the (main) program which up to now has included all statements between

- the first declaration and
- the statement END

Function subprograms having the following general form can be declared directly after the END statement of the main program:

```
type FUNCTION name(1fp)

        Declaration of the formal parameters (1fp) and all
        the variables used within the subprogram.

        Sequence of statements to calculate the value of
        the function.

name = ...
RETURN
END
```

The key word FUNCTION indicates that we are dealing with a function subprogram. The subprogram receives the name that follows the key word FUNCTION (indicated above by means of: "name"). The type of the function value to be calculated is defined by means of one of the key words CHARACTER, DOUBLE PRECISION, INTEGER, LOGICAL or REAL which replace "type", i.e. before the key word FUNCTION[*]. In order to transfer the calculated function values to a storage place, the name of the subprogram has to be specified in an appropriate declaration statement in that program segment where the call is made (main program or another subprogram).

---

[*] Only declarations of the type INTEGER, LOGICAL and REAL are allowed in the subset.

Formal parameters consist not only of (simple) variables but
also of vectors, matrices and other subprograms. The formal parameters represent storage place reservation for the actual parameters that are used when the function is called. It is, therefore, obvious that corresponding formal and actual parameters
must be of the same type.

The statement

        name = ...

in the above general form indicates that the calculated function
value has to be assigned to the name of the function subprogram.
The function value calculated using the actual parameters
occupies the storage place which belongs to this name. The
statement

        RETURN

following the calling of the subprogram and the calculation of
the functional value, results in "the return" to that program
segment where the call was made.

The RETURN statement does not necessarily have to be placed,
as implied, directly before the END statement. For example, it
can be sometimes useful if the return branch to the calling
program segment is dependent on a condition le. This can be
programmed as follows:

        IF(le) RETURN

The statement

        END

shows the end of the declaration of the subprogram. (It may be
used as an executable statement which can be skipped to if it
is provided with a label. This has the same effect as a RETURN
statement within the subprogram.)

The calling of a function subprogram can take place in the main
program or in other subprograms. This can take place in an
assignment statement, in an expression of the corresponding
type or in a WRITE statement in the output list (instead of a
variable, but this is not allowed in the subset).

All calls have the following points in common:

- name of the function subprogram and
- the actual parameter.

In order to illustrate the use of function subprograms the Example 7.1 will be slightly modified for the calculation of the Chebyshev polynomial.

Example 8.2

Calculate the 5th degree Chebyshev polynomial

$$y = 16x^5 - 20x^3 + 5x$$

using a function subprogram for the interval $[-1, 1]$ and a step length of 0.1.

The program solution will be first presented and then be explained.

```
      REAL X,Y,A(0:5)
      INTEGER J
      DATA (A(J), J=0,5,1) /0., 5., 0., -20., 0., 16./
      DO 1 X = -1,1.05,0.1
      WRITE (*,100) X,Y(X,A,5)
  100 FORMAT (1X,F6.2,F8.3)
    1 CONTINUE
      STOP
      END
```
main program

```
      REAL FUNCTION Y(X1,A1,N1)
      REAL X1,A1(0:N1),S
      INTEGER N1,J
      S = 0
      DO 1 J = N1,0,-1
      S = S*X1+A1(J)
    1 CONTINUE
      Y = S
      RETURN
      END
```
function subprogram y

Consideration of the function subprogram shows the function Y depends on the simple variables X1 and N1 as well as the vector A1. The subprogram has to be somehow informed that the parameter A1 is a vector. On the other hand, it is not advisable to fix the limits of the indices in the subprogram since they may vary with other actual parameters. The possibility is, therefore, available to include in the parameter list the (variable) limits of the vector as well as the name of the

vector. The following statement was thus made in the subprogram
of Example 8.2 above: [*]

```
    REAL A1(0:N1)
```

The auxiliary variable S in the subprogram Y is superfluous if
the intermediate results can be stored in the storage place
reserved for the function Y. The program could thus, for example,
have been written: [**]

```
    . . . .
    Y = 0
    DO 1 J = N1, 0, -1
    Y = Y*X1 + A1(J)
  1 CONTINUE
    RETURN
    END
```

The subprogram Y is called in the main program by means of the
WRITE statement using Y(X,A,5).

The actual parameters X, A and 5 are assigned to the formal
parameters X1, A1 and N1 respectively in the declaration of
subprogram Y. They replace those formal parameters in the subprogram, which are simply used to describe the subprogram. It
is, however, important that the corresponding parameters are
of the same type. For example the call

```
    Y(-1,A,5)
```

is _incorrect_, since the INTEGER constant -1 corresponds to the
formal parameter X1 which has the type REAL. The correct call
should be:

```
    Y(-1.,A,5)
```


A subprogram can be thought of as being a "black box".
What actually happens in the black box does not interest the
"outside world". We simply have the possibility - by means of

---

[*] 1) Variable index limits may only be used in subprograms in
connection of arrays as formal parameters.
2) For a more detailed description of the transfer of vectors
and matrices cf. page 82.

[**] This results in a subprogram not being able to call itself.
So-called recursive subprograms are not possible in Fortran.

the parameters - to input certain information into the box and finally obtain - by means of the name of the function subprogram - a certain value. Any other variables which are additionally required are unimportant outside of the subprogram. It is, therefore, allowed to use names for variables, vectors and matrices, required in the subprogram as auxiliary items in order to calculate the function values, which correspond to those names used in the main program or in other subprograms: These names are not connected with one another in any way whatsoever as they are considered as "local items". The same applies to the names of the formal parameters. They are also allowed to correspond to names used in other parts of the program.

It is now necessary to show how a function can be used as an argument of another subprogram. It is not enough to declare the name of the function as an actual parameter when calling the subprogram. In this case the function name would be interpreted as a simple variable and this would, of course, lead to an error. It must, therefore, be declared in the program segment in which the subprogram is called, that the name of the function has been defined as an additional subprogram "outside" of the program segment where the call is made. This takes place by means of the key word

EXTERNAL

followed by a list of all the names of subprograms written by the programmer which are used as actual parameters in a program call.[*)] Independent of this, however, the name of a function subprogram has to be listed in a declaration statement.

The above will now be illustrated by means of an example to calculate the integral value of a function by means of approximation.

Example 8.3

Calculate in the interval $[0, 1]$ the integral of the function

---

[*)] Note that the formula functions ("statement functions") and the predefined subprograms (cf. Appendix C, page 140) are not possible here. However, the subroutines described in the next chapter are allowed.

$$f(x) = x^2 - x + 1$$

by means of approximation using the trapezoid rule.

```
REAL A,B,TRAP,F,V          ⎤
EXTERNAL F                 ⎥   main program
.  .  .                    ⎥
V = TRAP(A,B,F)            ⎥
.  .  .                    ⎥
STOP                       ⎥
END                        ⎦

REAL FUNCTION F(X)         ⎤
REAL X                     ⎥   subprogram
F = X**2-X+1               ⎥      F
RETURN                     ⎥
END                        ⎦

REAL FUNCTION TRAP(X1,X2,FCT)       ⎤
REAL X1,X2,FCT                      ⎥   subprogram
TRAP = (FCT(X1)+FCT(X2))*(X2-X1)/2  ⎥      TRAP
RETURN                              ⎥
END                                 ⎦
```

Exercise 8.1

Determine the integral of the Chebyshev polynomial of
the fifth degree

$$y = 16\,x^5 - 2o\,x^3 + 5x$$

in the interval $[-1, 1]$ so that the error is not greater
than 10^{-6}. (Is the type REAL adequate enough for the
variables and functions used in order to obtain the required accuracy?).

Hint:

The following applies for the trapezoid rule

$$\int_a^b f(x)\ dx = \frac{b-a}{2}(f(a)+f(b))+R$$

with $\quad |R| \leqslant \dfrac{(b-a)^3}{12}\ \max_{x\in[a,b]} |f''(x)|$

whereby the estimation has to be carried out for every
partial interval.

Subprograms are provided for in Fortran for a large number of
mathematical functions. - They are considered as INTRINSIC
functions which can be called as if the function subprogram
had already been declared. Now there are large numbers of
functions which differ merely in the type of their argument
and in the resulting type of their function value such as, for
example, the absolute value: ABS, DABS and IABS (cf. Appendix C).
A common name is provided for such groups of functions and this
name defines the type of the function values dependent of the
type of the actual parameter. These functions are called
"generic" functions. (The subset does not provide for generic
functions).

A generic function loses its charateristic if it is used as an
actual parameter in the call of the subprogram. Over and above
this, predefined functions have to be listed as actual parameters
in an INTRINSIC statement instead of the EXTERNAL statement.
Since, however, there are some exceptions, it is recommended to
use, in general, the following procedure (in so far as it is
not necessary to pay attention to extremely effective programming):
The predefined function (INTRINSIC or GENERIC) is placed with
a new name in a function subprogram and this new function subprogram appears as an actual parameter as described.

Example: (cf. Example 8.3)

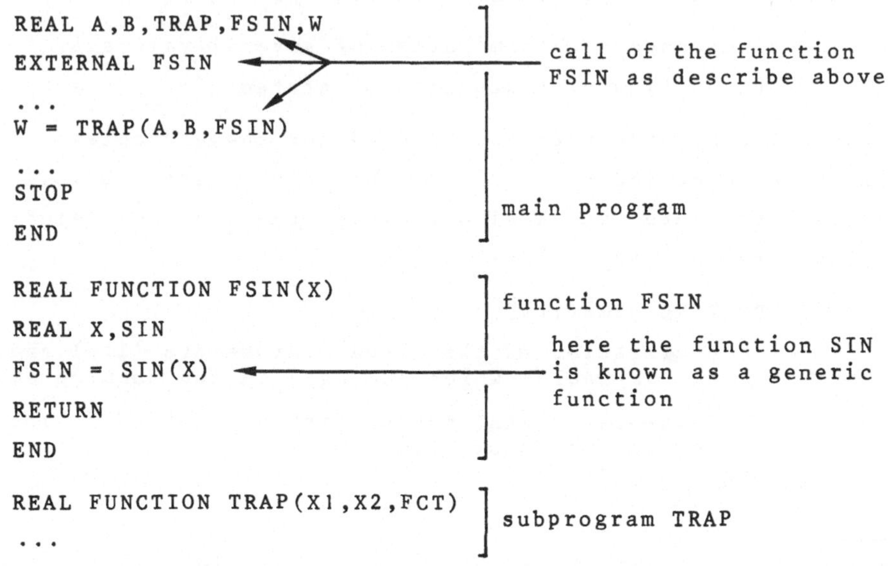

9 Subprogram Techniques: Subroutines; Vectors and Matrices as Parameters

The statement functions, the function subprograms and the pre-defined functions, whose application was dealt with in the previous chapter as well as in Appendix C, are used to calculate one function value from the given values of the arguments which are transferred to the subprogram as actual parameters.[*] Finally, the calculated function value is transferred back to the program segment where the call was made to a storage place having the name of the function subprogram.

Statements are allowed in function subprograms which cause side-effects when calculating the function value - such as, for example, input and output statements, modification of parameter values etc.. However, in the interest of orderly programming, which can easily be served, this would not be taken advantage of. The following limitations should be applied when using function subprograms:

- to transfer to the subprogram only those parameters which function values depend upon, and
- to transfer the calculated value to storage place of the function name in the program segment where the call is made.

There are a number of tasks which require

- simultaneous determination of several values or
- the uniting of a sequence of statements in a subprogram.

A special type of subprogram is used for these problems, namely, a so-called subroutine. Subroutines have the following general structure (which also includes the case for determining more than one value).

```
SUBROUTINE name(lfp)

    ⎡ Declaration of the formal parameters (lfp) and all
    ⎣ the variables which are used in the subprogram.

    ⎡ Sequence of statements which are united by the
    ⎣ name of the subroutine.

RETURN

END
```

[*] An additional possibility will be described in Chapter 10 in connection with the COMMON.

The key word

SUBROUTINE

indicates that all statements which follow up to the statements
RETURN and END form a program segment having the name which
directly follows the key word SUBROUTINE. This was illustrated
above by means of "name". The abbreviation lfp represents the
list of the formal parameters.

The flow of information via the parameter list need not only be
used to transfer information to the subroutine; a program call
can also cause to flow in the opposite direction, since it is
allowed to assign values to the formal parameters in a subprogram. The same parameter can be used for the exchange of information: However, because of reasons of orderly programming,
one should, where possible, use separate parameters for the
"input" to the subprograms and the "output" from them.

As opposed to function subprograms, it is not allowed to declare the name of a subroutine in the calling program. A function value is not transferred to a storage place having the
name of the subprogram; the name of the subroutine stands for
a sequence of statements which are to be executed with the
actual parameters when the subprogram is called. This first
implies that a subroutine has to be called in a different
manner to a function subprogram: The call takes place by means
of a special statement having the general form ('CALL
statement'):

CALL name(lap)

Once again lap represents the list of the actual parameters.
Subroutine statements are then processed, using these actual
parameters.

Exercise 9.1

Determine the zero position of the function

$$f(x) = \sin(x) - 0.2$$

in the interval $[0, \frac{\pi}{2}]$ using the halve step method.

Hint:

The function $f(x)$ is calculated in the middle of the interval using the halve step method. After this, the end

of the interval, which has the same sign as in the middle of the function, is replaced by the interval middle point. By means of continual halving, the interval converges to the desired zero position, if an interval boundary does not correspond to the zero position. The program solution of the above exercise can use the same parameter transfer as described in Chapter 8 (page 76) for variables and functions.

There are a large number of possible errors which can occur when transferring vectors and matrices to subprograms. These are very often difficult to recognize and can thus easily lead to incorrect results.

The first source of error results from the fact that a two or multi-dimensional matrix is internally stored and processed as a vector. This means that only a vector can be transferred to a subprogram independent of the number of indices - and their magnitude - declared for the matrix in the program segment where the call was made as well as the number of indices declared in the subprogram:

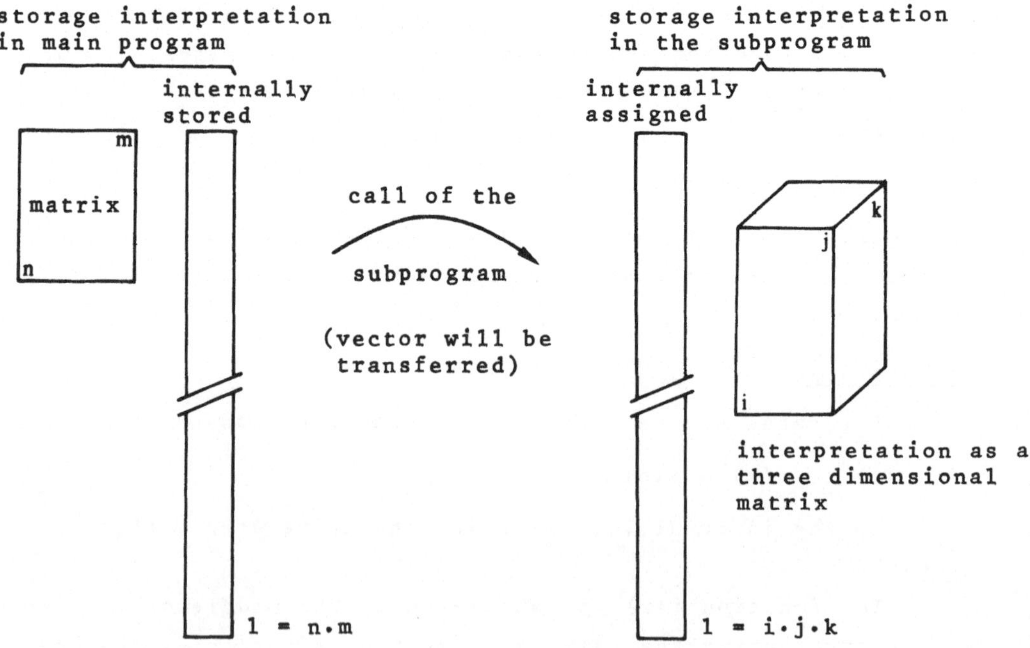

The - more formal - freedom to be able to define matrix forms
in the subprogram which are quite different to those in the
main program, causes difficulty in assigning values to the
appropriate vector places - by means of the appropriate matrix
elements. In practice one is never confronted with the dilemma
of choosing different dimensions for matrices when declaring
them and when calling a subprogram, one should, therefore, not
take advantage of the possibility described above.

Over and above this, when storing matrices in vector form
(cf. page 31), the number of rows of a matrix must be known
since the matrix is stored in columns. If the line number in
the main and subprogram differs, then the values of the matrix
are placed incorrectly as the following Example 9.1 shows.

Example 9.1

```
INTEGER A(3,4)    main        sub-        SUBROUTINE UP(B)
...               program     program     INTEGER B(2,4)
CALL UP(A)                                 ...
...
```

When the subprogram UP is called, the matrix A is transferred
in the following manner:

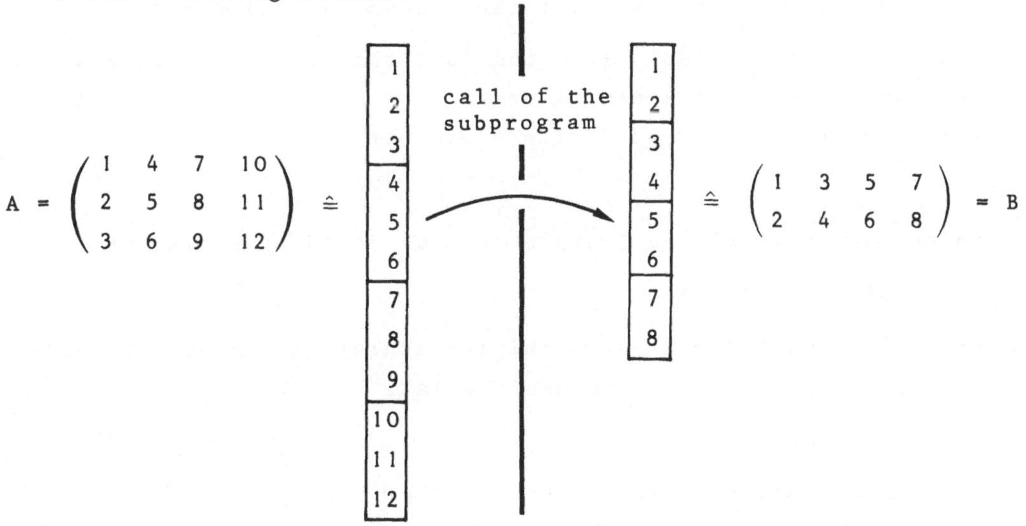

$$A = \begin{pmatrix} 1 & 4 & 7 & 10 \\ 2 & 5 & 8 & 11 \\ 3 & 6 & 9 & 12 \end{pmatrix} \;\hat{=}\; \begin{array}{|c|} \hline 1 \\ 2 \\ 3 \\ 4 \\ 5 \\ 6 \\ 7 \\ 8 \\ 9 \\ 10 \\ 11 \\ 12 \\ \hline \end{array} \xrightarrow{\text{call of the subprogram}} \begin{array}{|c|} \hline 1 \\ 2 \\ 3 \\ 4 \\ 5 \\ 6 \\ 7 \\ 8 \\ \hline \end{array} \;\hat{=}\; \begin{pmatrix} 1 & 3 & 5 & 7 \\ 2 & 4 & 6 & 8 \end{pmatrix} = B$$

For example, when executing the subprogram, the element

B(1,3)

does not receive the value of the element $A(1,3) = 7$, but rather the value of the element $B(1,3)$ in the vector which corresponds to 5.

On the other hand, however, since it is desirable to keep the index limits as a variable parameter, as different subprogram calls may require different matrices, the following conclusion should be drawn:

> Not only the name of a matrix but also the corresponding index limits should be transferred as parameters for every call of a subprogram.

Care must be taken that the limits defined in the declaration are transferred even then when only a part of the matrix is occupied. [*] The subprogram in Example 9.1 should have thus been as follows:

```
SUBROUTINE UP(B,N,M)
INTEGER N,M,B(N,M)
```

The call in the main program should have been:

```
CALL UP(A,3,4)
```

This would have resulted in the value of the element $B(1,3)$ corresponding to the value of the element $A(1,3)$ etc..

Further problems result from the fact that only one address is transferred to the storage area for the case of a vector or a matrix. Thus, instead of the statement

```
CALL UP(A)
```

in the program call of Example 9.1, we could have also written

```
CALL UP(A(1,1))
```

which implies that the same initial address is meant. It would have also been possible to use the call

```
CALL UP(A(3,1))
```

which would have resulted in the following:

---

[*] If the lower limits are not equal to 1, then they must have the same value in the main and subprogram or be transferred as a parameter (cf. vectors A and Al in Example 8.2, page 75).

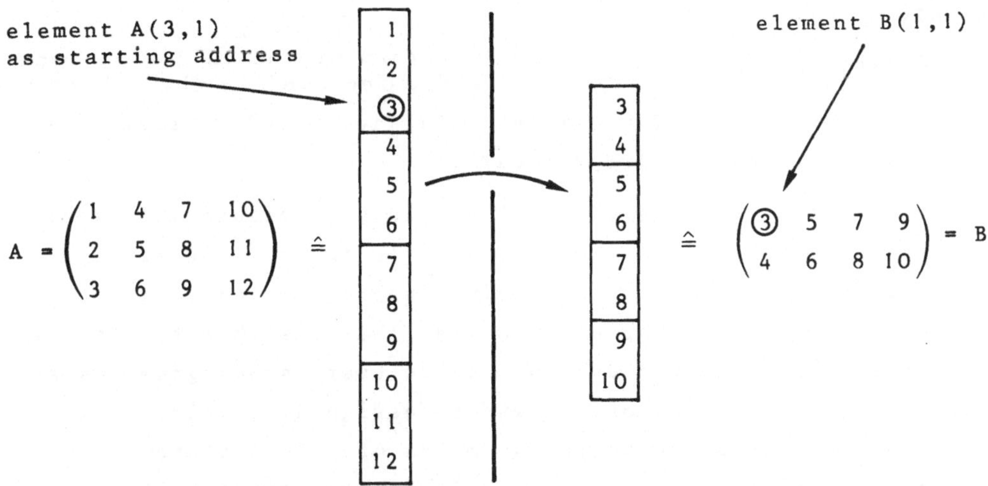

$$A = \begin{pmatrix} 1 & 4 & 7 & 10 \\ 2 & 5 & 8 & 11 \\ 3 & 6 & 9 & 12 \end{pmatrix} \hat{=} \qquad \hat{=} \begin{pmatrix} 3 & 5 & 7 & 9 \\ 4 & 6 & 8 & 10 \end{pmatrix} = B$$

In order to avoid this source of error, it is advisable to always write the names of the actual parameters for subprogram calls having vectors or matrices as arguments. Furthermore, a vector component or a matrix should only be used for the case that the corresponding formal parameter is a simple variable.

Exercise 9.2

> Write a subprogram which is capable of solving an
> equation system using Gauß' method (cf. Exercise 4.1,
> page 36). The given equation system should not be changed
> by the subprogram.

When dealing with certain problems, it is often useful to save a calculated value obtained by a subprogram (function subprogram or subroutine) call for the next subprogram. This can, of course, be done by means of an appropriate parameter[*] and is then very flexible for the individual subprogram calls – or by means of the statement SAVE which is possible in Fortran 77. The SAVE statement has to be declared in the subprogram and has the following general form:

        SAVE list

where list stands for the names of variables and fields which have to be separated by commas. If the list is empty, i.e.

[*] The same applies for the COMMON area which is described in the next chapter.

simply

```
      SAVE
```
| This form of the SAVE statement is not included in the subset

is declared, then - if possible - all fields and variables are saved for the next subprogram call.

In most Fortran compilers, local variables, vectors and matrices are arranged in a fixed area assigned in the working storage which corresponds to the respective subprograms and are not changed between two subprogram calls. They are thus treated as if the statement SAVE had been made in every subprogram. As a result of this, it is not allowed to assign an initial value to a variable in a subprogram by means of a DATA statement - since this initial value only applies to the first call of the subprogram -, if values are assigned to the variable later in the program. This, thus, leads to different results if the following assignments are made in the subprogram (cf. Example 8.2).

```
        S = 0.                          DATA S/0./
        DO 1 J=N1,0,-1                  DO 1 J=N1,0,-1
        S = S*X+A(J)                    S = S*X+A(J)
      1 CONTINUE                      1 CONTINUE
```

initial value 0. guaranteed for every call of the subprogram

initial value 0. guaranteed only for the first call of the subprogram

After calling and executing a subroutine, the program continues with the statement which directly follows the subroutine call. Now it is, however, possible that it is required to process different branches in the calling segment depending on the values calculated in the subroutine. The values calculated result in it being possible to distinguish between different cases (cf. page 23) in the calling program segment. (This way is recommended). The skip address can, however, be included in the subroutine call and the appropriate branch can then be skipped to directly from the subroutine. This requires a different form of the RETURN statement in the subprogram in conjunction with parameters in the subroutine call (full Fortran 77 only). In doing so, attention has to be paid to the following interaction:

1) Declaration of the subroutine:

   The statement

         SUBROUTINE name(lfp)

   results in the list of the formal parameters (cf. page 80)
   being extended by one or more asterisks (*). If a subroutine
   call is made later in the program, then a skip address can
   be declared at the position of one of the asterisks.

2) Several statements having the form

         RETURN n

   can be used within the subroutine. The value of n must be a
   positive integer number which is smaller or equal to the
   number of asterisks listed in the SUBROUTINE statement.

3) If the call of the subprogram has the form

         CALL name(lap)

   then skip addresses of the form

         *m

   have to be made in the list of actual parameters where an
   asterisk was placed in the declaration of the list of formal parameters. If the statement

         RETURN n

   is made in the subprogram, then that skip address is branched
   to which was given in the nth position of the list of actual
   parameters (in doing so, the other positions are not counted).

The following example will serve to illustrate this:

calling program section	subprogram
6 READ(...)...	SUBROUTINE UP(A,B,*,*,*)
CALL UP(X,Y,*6,*999,*40)	...
Z = 500	RETURN 1
...	...
40 WRITE(...)	K = 2
...	RETURN K
999 STOP	...
...	RETURN 3
	...
	RETURN
	END

After the subprogram has been called by means of CALL UP(...)
the following is executed:

- the READ statement having the statement number 6, if the
  statement RETURN 1 is processed in subprogram UP,

- the statement STOP having the statement number 999, if
  the variable K has the value 2 in the statement RETURN K,

- the WRITE statement having the number 40, if the statement RETURN 3 is processed,

- the statement Z = 500, if either the statement RETURN
  is reached in the subprogram or, if for one of the
  statements RETURN K the value of K is less than 1 or
  greater than 3, i.e. a skip address was not supplied
  (without error message).

In our opinion, it is not a particularly good method of programming to place the program control in a subprogram as
described above instead of in the main program. The program
remains more transparent if a variable is used as an indicator,
i.e. a value is assigned to it in the subprogram which is in
accordance with the desired result and this then causes the
branching in the program segment called to be dependent on the
value transferred. In this respect, the method of distinguishing
between different cases as was described in Chapter 3 (page 23)
can be used for the statement "computed GOTO". The latter case
requires that the variable used as an indicator is of the
type INTEGER.

The "computed GOTO" statement has the general form:

    GOTO (lsn) k

where

    lsn stands for the list of statement numbers and
    k   stands for a variable of the type INTEGER.

If the list lsn consists of n statement numbers, e.g. $m_1, m_2, \ldots, m_n$
some of which may be equal, then the program branches to the
statement having the number m_j, if k possesses the value j.
If k is smaller than 1 or greater than n, then the computed

GOTO statement is ignored, i.e. it has the same effect as a CONTINUE statement and the program continues with the next statement.

Appropriate value assignments to a variable could have been made in the above example instead of the RETURN n statements. The example would then have been as follows:

calling program section	subprogram

```
calling program section          subprogram

                                 SUBROUTINE UP(A,B,N)
      ...                        N = 0
                                 ...
    6 READ (...)...              N = 1
      ...                        RETURN
      CALL UP(X,Y,K)             ...
      GOTO (6,999,40) K          N = 2
      Z = 500                    RETURN
      ...                        ...
   40 WRITE                      N = 3
      ...                        RETURN
  999 STOP                       ...
      ...                        N = 0
                                 RETURN
                                 END
```

10 Parameter Transfer by Means of the COMMON Statement

The last two chapters described how information can be exchanged between the calling part of the program and the subprogram being called. In addition to these possibilities, a storage area can be defined which can be accessed not only from the main program but from all subprograms. This mutual storage area is the so-called COMMON area.

Before we illustrate how the COMMON is defined and how it can be accessed, it is necessary to look into which information is required in order to reserve this area. In doing so 3 points have to be taken into account:

1) Where does the common storage area start? Or in other words: What is the name of the first storage place of the COMMON area?

2) How big should the COMMON area be?

3) What kind of structure should the COMMON area have?

The above information is passed on to the computer by means of a single instruction, the so-called COMMON statement, whereby certain amount of information is provided by the declaration statement. An example based only on the main program will be used to illustrate this.

Example 10.1

```
DOUBLE PRECISION A,B,C ,D(3,2)
INTEGER N,M,I,K
COMMON A,D,N,K,I
```

By means of the above, a COMMON area is defined which begins with the variable A. It contains the variable A, the matrix elements D(1,1), D(2,1),...,D(3,2) and the variables N, K and I in a consecutive series.

A	D(1,1)	D(2,1)	D(3,1)	D(1,2)	D(2,2)	D(3,2)	N	K	I

The variable A and the matrix D were declared as DOUBLE PRECISION items, i.e. they require 2 words, thus the total COMMON area requires 7 * 2 + 3 = 17 storage places. The length of the COMMON area results from the sum of the storage places required

by the individual items (variables, vectors and matrices).[*]
At the same time the addition of the individual items in the
COMMON statement defines the structure of the area.

Almost all computers require that the data types using
DOUBLE PRESISION begin at a so-called double word alignment.[**]
This is automatically accepted by the Fortran compiler. If it
is necessary to have a double word in the middle of a COMMON
area, then this can lead to gaps of one word length. If the
COMMON structure in a subprogram deviates from that in the main
program, then these gaps can lead to an incorrect assignment
(different subprograms can be provided with different structures
of the COMMON area, see below). It is therefore advisable to
apply the following sequence of variable types when defining
the COMMON area:[***]

> 1) All items of the type DOUBLE PRECISION (or COMPLEX).
> 2) All items of the type INTEGER, LOGICAL or REAL.

It is not permitted in Fortran 77 to combine items of the type
CHARACTER with items of another type in one COMMON area. This
results from the different length definitions.

If such items should share a common storage area in a subprogram (function subprogram or subroutine), then the same declarations have to be made in the subprogram as described above.
Once again a COMMON statement defines how the first storage
place of the COMMON area should be called, how big the area
should be and what type of structure it should possess. Hence,
the following sequence of statements

```
SUBROUTINE UP1(X)
REAL X
DOUBLE PRECISION Y(3),Z(3),X1
INTEGER J,M,L
COMMON X1,Y,Z,J,L,M
...
```

in addition to the statements in Example 10.1, results in the

---

[*] Deviations can result if attention is not paid to the sequence
necessary for storage of the various variable types (cf. below).
[**] The same applies for the variable type COMPLEX which is described
in the next chapter.
[***] This is only required in full Fortran 77, since the data types
DOUBLE PRECISION and COMPLEX are not available in the subset.

following:

main program
interpretation

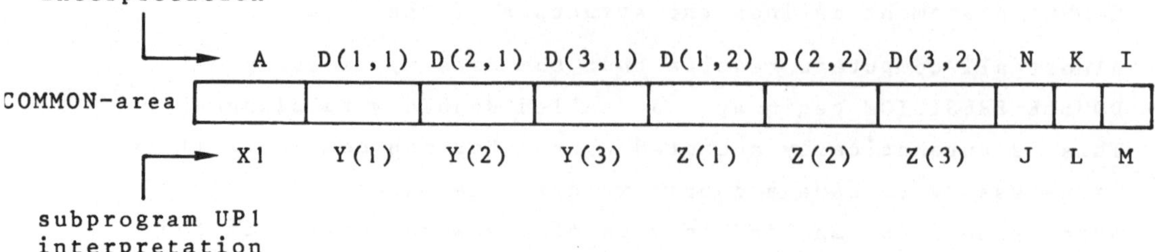

These different methods of interpretation result in the following:

The variables A,N,K,I or the matrix elements D(1,1),...,D(3,2)
in the main program are assigned values and respective storage
places in the COMMON area are given these values.

If the subroutine UP1 is then called by means of a CALL statement, then the names X1,Y(1),..,Y(3),Z(1),..,Z(3),J,L and M
possess the previously assigned values of the COMMON area. A
number of values have thus been transferred to the subprogram
in a manner which is not normally possible using the list of
formal and actual parameters: Matrix D in the main program has
been transformed into the vectors Y and Z in the subprogram.

Since it is also possible to assign values to the variables of
the COMMON area in the subprogram, the flow of information can
take place in the opposite direction. This, of course, also
takes place when several subprograms share the COMMON area. In
doing so, the same method applies as was described above.

It is formally allowed not only to give different structures to
matrices and vectors of the COMMON area in the main program and
subprogram, but also to the individual storage place. For
example, the storage place of the double word variable A of the
main program can be interpreted in the subprogram as two consecutive variables V1 and V2 (of type INTEGER, REAL, or LOGICAL).
Since this technique can easily lead to errors which cannot be
recognized by the computer and as there are only a few possibilities of application which require a different interpretation of the structure of the COMMON area in the main and subprogram, it is advisable, especially for beginners, to always use

the same structure (also the individual variables) when defining the COMMON area in the main and subprogram. Over and
above this, it is recommended to simply copy the COMMON statements of the main program and use them in the various subprograms (inclusive of the respective declaration statement). This
ensures that the COMMON area in the various program sections
has an identical structure.

The COMMON area is not only used for the interchange of information between various program segments, but also for
mutual superimposition of local items in the various subprograms. This enables the saving of space in the working storage.

Example:

main program: A   D(1,1)...D(3,2)   N   K   I

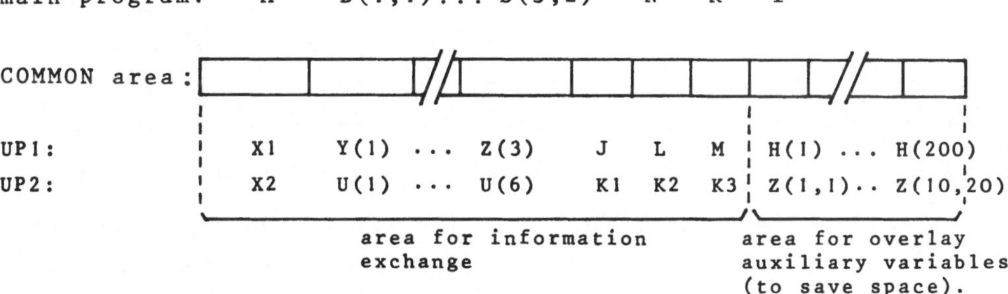

In Fortran programs, it is, of course, not immediately notice-
able if one part of the COMMON area is used for the interchange of information between the main and subprograms or between the various subprograms, and another part of the COMMON
area is merely used to save space ("overlay") in the various
subprograms. In this respect, the comment lines should be used
to give a clear indication.

COMMON areas can also be provided with a name. The name of the
area is declared in the COMMON statement between slashes (division sign) and includes all storage places in the COMMON block
that are declared after the name. Hence

        COMMON /B1/A,B,C

defines a COMMON block with the name B1 which consists of the
variables A, B and C. If it is required to define several
storage areas and to provide them with names, then the name of

the next block follows the last storage place of the previous block and is inserted between two slashes. If it is required to use a combination of "labeled COMMON" and "unlabeled COMMON" areas then the unlabeled area has to be declared first.

Hence, the declaration:

COMMON X,Y,Z,Z1/B1/A,B,C/B2/C1,C2

it is advisable to use the declarations

```
COMMON X,Y,Z,Z1
COMMON /B1/ A,B,C
COMMON /B2/ C1,C2
```

creates three different COMMON areas, namely,

- the unlabeled COMMON area with the items X,Y,Z,Z1
- the COMMON block with the name B1 and the items A,B,C and
- the COMMON block with the name B2 and the items C1 and C2.

Whereas the unlabeled COMMON area is inserted in the main program, the labeled COMMON area can be used for the interchange of information between the various subprograms without reserving an area in the main program. This can be an advantage when using the "overlay technique" for a complicated program.

If a variable is included in a COMMON area, then it is not permitted to initialize this variable (by means of a DATA statement, cf. page 67). A reason for this restriction is that different initializations in the various subprograms can lead to contradictory initial conditions. It is only possible to carry out an initialization with the BLOCK DATA subprogram for labeled COMMON areas.[*] It has the same structure as the declaration of a subprogram (hence the name) and has to be declared at a corresponding position, i.e. not in other program segments.

Since the initialization of the variables with values takes place during the translation of the program, the "calling" of the BLOCK DATA subprogram is not provided for and, as a result, a name is not required. If, however, it is declared, then the only effect is to document the program. Thus the BLOCK DATA subprogram has the following general form:

---

[*] The BLOCK DATA statement is not included in the subset, i.e. initialization of the COMMON area cannot take place during compilation.

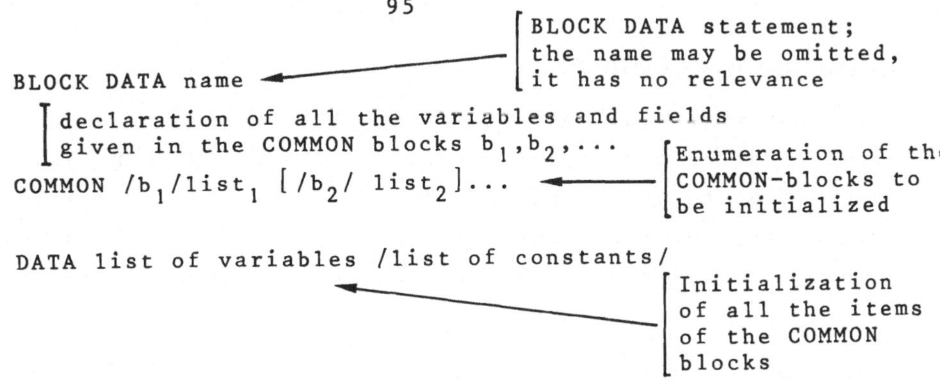

When initializing the items of the labeled COMMON area $b_1, b_2, \ldots$, it is important that all the variables in the DATA statement receive initial values.

It has been shown that the COMMON statement can be used to create different structures in the main and subprograms (cf. page 92). Furthermore, it is possible for each individual storage place to be interpreted in a different manner by means of defining different types for corresponding storage places of the common area in the subprogram and main program. The EQUIVALENCE statement is a similar possibility which enables, within a particular program segment, reference to the same storage place with different variable names and also with different types. This has the general form:

    EQUIVALENCE (variable list) $[$,(variable list)$]\ldots$

where variable list represents at least two variable names separated by commas which refer to the same storage place. Additional names can be declared in an EQUIVALENCE statement which refer to other storage places in the same manner. This is implied above by the following general form:

    $[$,(variable list) $]$ ...

It is of particular importance to know how the individual variables are internally stored when variables of different types are used to access the same storage place. It is, therefore, recommended to consult the respective hand books of the computer in use. In general, use of the EQUIVALENCE statement causes great difficulty when trying to run the same program on different computers. Hence, this statement should be used as little as possible (indeed, we doubt if it is at all necessary).

11 The Data Type COMPLEX

Up to now when dealing with arithmetic expressions we have only considered the data types DOUBLE PRECISION, INTEGER, and REAL. In addition to this, full Fortran 77 is capable of dealing with arithmetic expressions containing complex values.[*] In general, complex numbers are represented by the following forms:

$$z = x+iy \qquad \text{with} \quad i = \sqrt{-1}$$

In Fortran, complex values are arranged in pairs of values:

$$z = (x, y)$$

where

    x represents the real part and
    y represents the imaginary part.

The items x and y both possess the storage form REAL and this is how they appear in the working storage.[**] Variables of the type COMPLEX have to be included in a declaration statement of the following general form:

    COMPLEX list of variables

The variable list not only applies to simple variables but also vectors and matrices whereby the limits for the indices have to be specified. This can take place - as already described - either directly after the declaration of the name or in a special

    DIMENSION statement | (cf. page 34)

Fortran 77 not only provides for variables of the type COMPLEX as described above but also complex constants. These are written in the form of a pair of values (see above) whereby both constants possess the type REAL or in addition INTEGER.

For example, the constant

    (3.14, -1)

represents the complex value 3.14-i. The INTEGER component is internally transformed into an item of the type REAL. In this

---

[*] The data type COMPLEX is not included in the subset.

[**] Double precision complex numbers are not provided for in Fortran 77; many computers do, however, have the higher accuracy.

respect, however, attention must be paid to the possibility of
a loss of accuracy.

The following table defines the arithmetic operations that can
take place between two items (variable or constant)

and
$$z = (x,y) \quad \hat{=} \quad x+iy$$
$$c = (a,b) \quad \hat{=} \quad a+ib$$

of the type COMPLEX:

meaning		operation	result
addition subtraction $\}$	$z\pm c$	$(x,y)\pm(a,b)$	$(x\pm a,\ y\pm b)$
multiplication	$z\star c$	$(x,y)\star(a,b)$	$(x\star a-y\star b,\ x\star b+y\star a)$
division	z/c	$(x,y)/(a,b)$	$((x\star a+y\star b)/(a\star a+b\star b),$ $(a\star y-x\star b)/(a\star a+b\star b))$

In addition, exponentiation in the form of $z\star\star c$ is provided for
and there are a number of predefined functions for complex
parameters in Fortran programs (cf. Appendix C).

Complex numbers containing items of the type INTEGER and REAL
may be combined in an arithmetic expression.[*] The result is
of the type COMPLEX and the value corresponds to the chosen
operation (within the framework of the possible number representation). In order to input and output complex values, no
special format code is provided and the format codes for the
real and imaginary components have to be defined in the same
manner as for items of the type REAL, namely,[**]

    rDw.d
    rEw.d
    rFw.d

---

[*] A connection between the types COMPLEX and DOUBLE PRECISION is
not provided for in Fortran 77. Nevertheless, a lot of computers
do allow for this possibility.

[**] Care should be taken that the possible use of the format code D
does not lead to an incorrect interpretation: The numbers are
stored internally as single precision and not double precision.

12 File Access

In chapters 5 and 6 it was described how to output data by
means of the printer and also how to input data. In order to
do this, the WRITE statement (cf. page 38) and two types of
the READ statement (cf. page 52 and 58) in conjunction with
format declarations were described. The experience gained will
now be extended to "files".

A file consists of a large amount of data required for a certain task and is stored on a peripheral device of a computer.
For example, this can be an output list or a series of input
lines.

It would not be economic to transfer individual items of data
to a peripheral storage device or to read them from it, and as
a result several items of data are combined to form a "record".
This combination is achieved at the program level by means of
the READ or WRITE statement. A data input line or an output
line can be thought of as being a record.

Over and above this, at the level of the control statement a
number of records can be combined to form a "data block". The
respective data blocks are then transferred to the external
data devices. The operating system automatically converts the
records to data blocks which means that the user need only be
concerned with records when considering Fortran programs.

In the files we have considered up to now (standard input,
printer output), records were transferred one after the other
and processed. This type of file organization is called as
"sequential" file or a "file with sequential access". In
addition to the standard input and output described up to now,
file organization can also take place on magnetic data devices
(magnetic tape, magnetic disk). A "direct access file" is one
where every record can be accessed independently of the others,
i.e. it has an address. It is obvious that this can only take
place on magnetic disks and not on magnetic tapes.

Before any details are presented regarding the access of data
in Fortran which has been stored on a magnetic data device,
we shall illustrate how data can be stored on a magnetic tape
or a magnetic disk.

A magnetic tape is a plastic foil an inch wide which has a
magnetic surface. The standard lengths are approximately 360
meters and 720 meters. Modern magnetic tape devices are capable
of writing on nine-track magnetic tapes: From these nine tracks,
eight correspond to the 8 bits of a byte. The ninth track is
used for recording a control bit (parity bit) which is placed
in such a manner that the number of bits is uneven. Control
bits are used to help find damaged areas on a tape or transfer
errors.

<u>Example:</u>

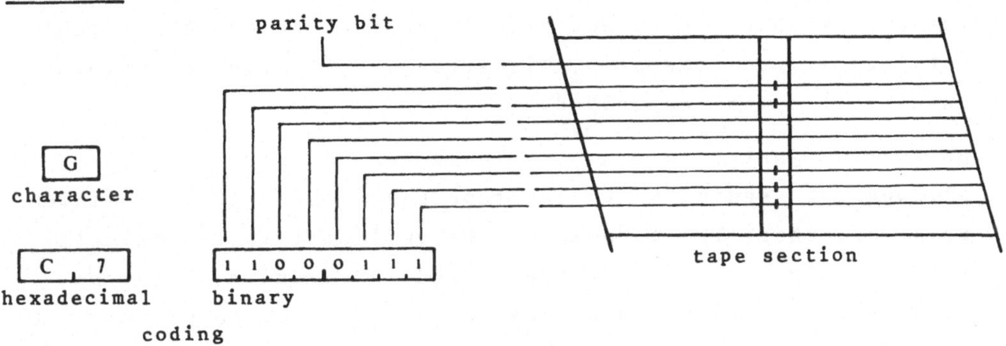

The density of recording on a magnetic tape is 800, 1600, or
6250 bpi ("bits per inch"). Since a character or byte is
written in a parallel manner on a magnetic tape, 800, 1600 or
6250 characters are stored per inch.

The magnetic tape station can only transfer data to the magnetic
tape if the tape passes the read stations at the correct
velocity. Approximately 0.7 cm $\sim \frac{1}{3}$ inch of tape is required
for the starting and stopping of the tape. The length of tape
required for acceleration cannot be used for the storage of
data and it is considered as a block gap or an "internal
record gap". A maximum of 30 million characters can be stored
on a long magnetic tape having a recording density of 1600 bpi,
depending on the number of characters in the data blocks
which are transferred as a unit to the magnetic tape.

It is quite possible that a file only takes up a fraction of
a magnetic tape and as a result, several files can be stored
on the same tape. In general, users of computers do not wish

to be confronted with the organization of data storage on magnetic tapes. Instead it is expected that this takes place automatically. Thus, for example, the magnetic tape should be automatically positioned at the first data block of an existing file which has to be read, no matter if the file in question is the first one on the tape.

The above requirements mean, on the one hand, that there has to be a file organization system incorporated in the operating system and on the other hand, additional information to the data to be stored on the magnetic tape. In order to acquaint the user with how this additional information and the actual data are stored, the principle structure of files on magnetic tapes will now be described.

On every magnetic tape a certain length of spare tape is allowed for feeding on to the tape heads and this is followed by a reflector. The purpose of the reflector is to optically indicate the beginning of the stored information. A second reflector is positioned at the end of the tape to prevent the whole tape being completely drawn through.

The first block after the first reflector mark contains the "volume header label". The volume label, as it is usually abbreviated, contains all important information regarding the tape number and the user. If the volume header label is deleted, then all files on the tape are lost. Therefore, in order to minimize this danger, the volume label should only be created by the staff of a computer center.

The volume label is followed by a second block which contains the "file header label" or "header 1". This block contains the following information about the file:

    - the name (up to 17 characters)
    - the date of creation
    - the release date.

The information about the structure of the data within the data blocks is contained in the "header 2". This information refers to

    - the length of the data block ("block length")
    - the length of the data record ("record length"),

i.e. the number of characters per data block and data record.
Some operating systems do not create the header 2 or evaluate
it. In such cases, the information has to be given by appropriate control statements.

The area in which the various labels are declared is separated
from the actual data area by means of a so-called "tape mark".
The data blocks are followed by the so-called trailer label.
The EOF1 mark ("end of file trailer label") is placed first
and contains the number of the data blocks as well as the same
information on file label header 1. The EOF2 mark which then
follows contains the same information as the label header 2.
If the file is the only one on the tape then the EOF2 mark is
followed by two tape marks. They indicate that no further data
is on the tape.

If, on the other hand, there is at least one additional file,
then only one tape mark is placed and it is followed by label
header 1 and header 2 of the next file. [*)]

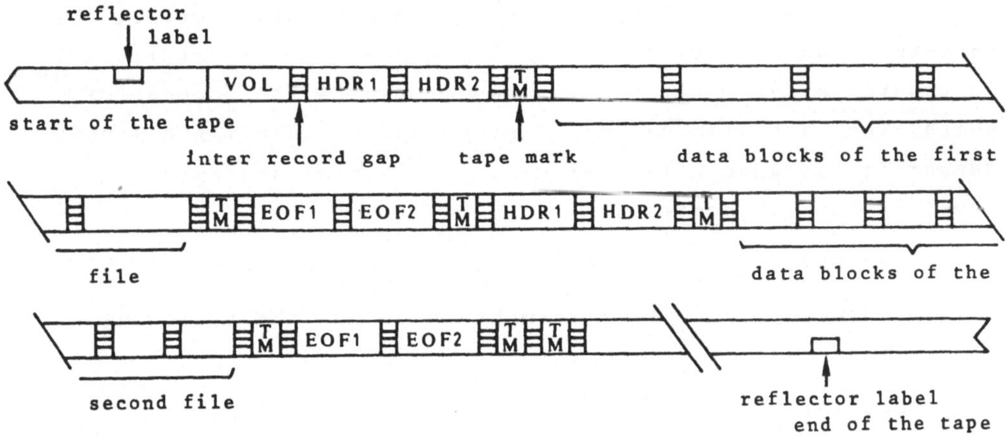

Since the various files are stored one after the other, a file
can only be modified, (i.e. deleted or extended by means of
additional data) if it is the last in the series of files. If
a file is modified then the following files are lost.

[*)] The operating system can create additional, non-standardized
tape labels.

If a sequential file (for instance on a magnetic tape) is transferred to a magnetic disk, then the operating system of the computer organizes the file structure including the two file labels and the two trailer labels in the same manner. Since the disk continually rotates and does not require to be accelerated to the prescribed velocity for data transfer, this does not require the block gaps needed on magnetic tapes. Over and above this, a previously created file can be extended, deleted or totally overwritten without the other files being affected - as is the case for magnetic tapes. Apart from these differences, files on magnetic tapes and disks can be handled in the same manner: They represent sequential files in the processing program which are either read, created or extended. Alternative reading and writing of individual data records is not allowed and is only possible for direct access files which, in turn, can only be organized on a magnetic disk.

Due to historical reasons, the Fortran programming language deals with "units" instead of "files". The units can be directly contacted by means of the unit number. In the framework of a more general operating system concept, however, the (external) unit is replaced by the file which was described in general above. What remains in Fortran is the concept of units: They are also called "logical units". The logical unit number is assigned a file by means of control statements at the level of the job control.

All files have to be opened before they can be accessed.

This is done by the OPEN statement which has the following form:

```
OPEN(u)
```

The number of the logical unit is represented by u which causes the associated file to be opened. Another form of the OPEN statement with additional parameters is given on page 107 where direct access files are dealt with.

The statements READ and WRITE enable all kinds of file accesses regardless if they have been organized in a "sequential" or "direct form". These statements have the general form:

READ (control information) input list |*)

for the input statement and for the output statement:

WRITE (control information) output list |*)

Control information is given in the form of a list. The first position of the list contains

the "logical unit"

and the second position contains

the number of the corresponding format.

All further control information is provided for by means of key words in the third position. Up to now this has been used to indicate the end condition for input in the form of

END=m

Apart from this, the following key words can be used:

ERR = s
IOSTAT = v   ] Not allowed in the subset
REC = r

They have the following meaning:

1) ERR = s

If a transfer error occurs during the input or output of data, then the transfer of data is interrupted and the program branches to the statement having the number s.

2) IOSTAT = v

An INTEGER variable (or the component of an INTEGER field) is represented by v. After the input or output operation the variable v is assigned a value which can provide information about the status of the transfer operation. The following standard values are provided for:

v = 0 : the transfer has taken place correctly.

v > 0 : a transfer error has taken place. (specification of the various error code depends on the compiler).

v < 0 : the end of the file has been reached.

---

*) The input and output lists may be empty; in such a case, a data record is either ignored (input) or a record without a variable value is output (if necessary empty for the case that the corresponding format does not contain a text constant).

Instead of the two declarations END=... and ERR=..., information concerning the status of the transfer can be obtained using the key word IOSTAT=v and this can be followed by branching depending on the value of the variable v.

3) REC = r

This third type of declaration is only for those files having direct access. The record, i.e. the data record, which is to be either read or written, has to be specified. In doing so r represents an arithmetic expression having an integer value (full language version; in the subset version r is represented by an INTEGER constant or an INTEGER variable).

In order to achieve a uniform representation of control information, the full language version of Fortran 77 provides additional key words for the logical unit and for the format statement. These are

    UNIT = u   for the logical unit
    FMT = f   for the format statement.

If the above key words are used, then it is not necessary to declare the logical unit u and the format having the number f in the first or second position of the control information respectively.

After all the data has been transferred, output files have to be ended with an 'end of file' mark. This can be done using the following statement:

    ENDFILE u   (u: Number of the logical unit).

Finally - or in the case of an input file after reading the data - the files have to be closed. This is done by the statement: [*)]

    CLOSE (u)
or   CLOSE (UNIT = u)

whereby u represents the file to be closed.

[*)] The CLOSE statement is not included in the subset; nevertheless, some of the compilers used by small computers require this statement in order to close a file; the parameter STATUS = 'KEEP' is then important.

The CLOSE statement can be used for the declaration of additional
control information such as the key words ERR=s and IOSTAT=v
described above for the READ and WRITE statements. This is, however, of secondary importance. The following two key words are,
though, of importance in the CLOSE statement:

STATUS = 'KEEP'   or   STATUS = 'DELETE'

These statements determine the status of the file after termi-
nation of the program: If 'KEEP' is given, then the file is
saved whilst 'DELETE' results in it being deleted. In order to
delete a file, it is, however, recommended to do this in a
special run using the so-called service programs ("utilities")
and as a result we shall not discuss this here in details.

If the above statement concerning the closing of a file is not
explicitly made, then the file is automatically closed at the
end of the program. The statement is, thus, not absolutely
necessary. It does, however, enable the operating system to
free the unit (magnetic tape or magnetic disk station) at an
early stage.

Certain problems sometimes require that the magnetic tape be
returned to the start of the file within a program execution -
or in general terms, to also include sequential magnetic disk
files - to the first data record. This is carried out by the
statement

REWIND u   (u: Number of the logical unit).

If it is required to only go back one data record (for example
to read the record once again) then the statement

BACKSPACE u

can be used. If it is required to go back several data records,
then the corresponding number of BACKSPACE statements have to
be made. [*)]

Exercise 12.1

Write a program capable of combining two similar sequential files having sorted data into a new file also
having sorted data.

____

[*)] Pay attention that the nonuniform writing of BACKSPACE, ENDFILE
and REWIND does not require parentheses in the subset, whilst
the other statements - OPEN, READ, WRITE, (CLOSE) do require them.

Having described the basics of the processing of sequential
files, we will now discuss how direct access files are processed.

In general, only files having fixed record lengths, i.e. not
variable record lengths, are allowed to be accessed directly
in Fortran 77. Individual data records are given numbers
when the file is created, and it is by means of these numbers
that the data record can be accessed at a later date. This
form of the file with direct access can, thus, be thought of as
having all data records - similar to the component of a vector
- one after the other. In a similar manner to the index of a
vector, every data record can be called or transferred to an
addressed area by means of appropriately placing the value r
after the key word REC in the READ or WRITE statement (see
above page 104). Every data transfer can, thus, take place independently of all other data records which have been read or
written.

Although the respective record numbers are stored in the file,
the Fortran program only supplies the contents of the data
records. In addition to this - for reasons of optimizing the
access which was described above - several data records are
combined to form a data block. Furthermore, this block contains extra control information which is automatically organized by the operating system. In general, direct access files
can be represented by the following illustration:

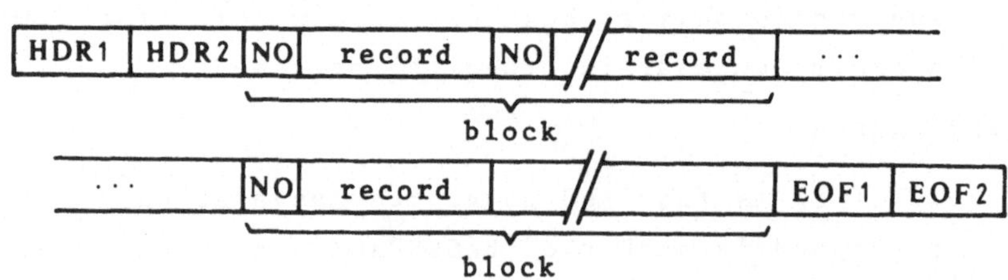

The subset version only allows for non-formated direct access
files. This means that information concerning the format
numbers is omitted in the READ and WRITE statements.

A direct access file u of record length l requires following
statement:

Open the file:

```
OPEN(u, ACCESS = 'DIRECT', RECL = 1)
```

Read the data from the data record having the number r
and transfer to the input list "list"

```
READ(u, REC = r) list
```

Write the data from the output list "list" and transfer
to the data record having the number r:

```
WRITE(u, REC = r) list
```

The full language version of Fortran 77 allows the use of
formatted as well as unformatted files. The user has to distinguish between the two possibilities in the OPEN statement.
This is done by means of the statement

```
FORM = 'FORMATTED'
```

or alternatively

```
FORM = 'UNFORMATTED'
```

Over and above this, the OPEN statement can be used to define
the status of the file (STATUS = 'NEW', 'OLD', 'SCRATCH' or
'UNKNOWN') and its name (FILE = '...'). Since larger computers
usually use control statements to achieve this, we will not go
into it in any further detail.

Exercise 12.2

When dealing with personal data, it is recommended to
separate that data directly related to persons, (i.e.
name, address) from the other data, (i.e. salary, allowances,
deductions) and to store this data in separate files.
This can take place by means of two direct access files
whereby the record number of each data record in the file
is included in the corresponding record of the other file.
It thus creates a link between the two files.
Write a program capable of listing the data stored in the
two files.

Some problems require that the records of a sequential file
are read using different kinds of formats. In doing so the
decision regarding which format to use can depend on the information in the data record which is just being read. This problem can only be solved in Fortran if there is a possibility
to interpret the data record according to different formats.
This can take place in Fortran 77 in the following form:

1) The data record is transferred to a variable of type
   CHARACTER*n as an intermediate buffer. Use the format
   code Aw.

2) The information which is required for the choice of
   format is then read from the intermediate buffer.

3) The intermediate buffer is read once again and interpreted according to the chosen format.

Since the intermediate buffer in the working storage is a
variable of type CHARACTER and the data is read by means of a
READ statement, it is considered as an 'internal READ statement'
as opposed to the READ considered up to now which merely read
external files. Furthermore, in this respect the CHARACTER
variable is called an 'internal file'. This general form of
the internal READ statement is:

    READ (v,f) input list
  f FORMAT (format codes, as described in chapter 6)

The v is a variable of the type CHARACTER having appropriate
length and data.

Example:

    The address of the receiver of an invoice is characteri-
    zed in a sequential file in a data record by means of
    the letter 'A' in position 1. The supplied goods are
    characterized in the following data records by means of
    the letter 'G' being stored in position 1. Carry out an
    appropriate analysis of the data records making assumptions
    about the remaining partitioning of the data records.

```
      CHARACTER*80 RECORD
      CHARACTER*1 C
      CHARACTER*15 NAME,STREET,CITY
      REAL QUANTITY,COST

      OPEN(u,...)

      READ(u,100,END=...) RECORD
  100 FORMAT(A80)
      READ(RECORD,101)C
  101 FORMAT(A1)
      IF(C .EQ. 'A') THEN
      READ(RECORD,102) NAME, STREET, CITY
  102 FORMAT(1X,3A15)
      ...
      ELSE
      IF(C .NE. 'G')      error message
      READ(RECORD,103) QUANTITY, COST
  103 FORMAT(1X,F5.1,F8.2)
      ...
      END IF
      ...
```

On the other hand, it is sometimes desirable to prepare the
data in a variable of the type CHARACTER and transfer the result then to a file, (i.e. direct access file which has to be
unformatted in the subset version). The 'internal WRITE statement' is provided for this task in Fortran 77 and has the
general form:

```
      WRITE(v,f) output list
    f FORMAT (format code as described in chapter 5)
```

where v is a variable of the type CHARACTER having an appropriate length.

Solutions to the Examples and the Exercises

The solutions illustrated in this chapter are identical to those carried out on an actual computer. Of course, the particular characteristics of the computer and the compiler have to be taken into account. Moreover, programming exercises can often be solved in a number of different ways and as a result, the programs described here are merely intended to show the user a possible solution and serve for checking purposes.

Example 1.1 (page 4) and Exercise 1.1 (page 9)

```
C  EXAMPLE 1.1, EXERCISE 1.1
       REAL A,B,M
       A = 1.4
       B = 2.1
       M = (A+B)/2.0
       WRITE (*,100) A,B,M
   100 FORMAT (1X,5F15.6)
       STOP
       END
```

The following results were printed:

       1.400000   2.100000   1.750000

Exercise 1.2 (page 9)

```
C  EXERCISE 1.2
       REAL A,B,C,S,F
       A = 2.
       B = 3.5
       C = 4.
       S = (A+B+C)/2.
       F = (S*(S-A)*(S-B)*(S-C))**0.5
       WRITE (*,100) A,B,C,F
   100 FORMAT (1X,5F15.6)
       STOP
       END
```

$\underline{A}$	$\underline{B}$	$\underline{C}$	$\underline{F}$
2.000000	3.500000	4.000000	3.499443

The result obtained for F corresponds, within the range of accuracy, to the correct value of 3.5.

<u>Exercise 2.1 (page 14)</u>

```
C  EXERCISE 2.1
      REAL A,B,C,D
      INTEGER J,K,N
      K = 12345                    <--------    [alternative:
      J = 10                                    [K = 1234567890
      A = J**(-2)                               [for main frame computer
      B = J**(-2.)
      C = K*5/J
      D = K*(5/J)
      N = (K+0.)*5/J
      WRITE (*,100) A,B,C,D,N
  100 FORMAT (1X,4F16.6,I11)
      STOP
      END
```

The results printed by the computer were:

micro processor:

A	B	C	D	N
.000000	.010000	-381.000000	.000000	6172

main frame computer:

A	B	C	D	N
.000000	.010000	617283800.000000	.000000	617283584

Although the first two values printed and the last 3 should be
the same, they are, however, different.

<u>Variable A:</u>	The exponentiation results from $\frac{1}{j*j}$. The
A = J**(-2)	INTEGER division results in the value 0 .

<u>Variable B:</u>	An operand has the type REAL (constant 2.),
B = J**(-2.)	hence the intermediate result is of the type
	REAL and coincides with the expected value.

<u>Variable C:</u>	The product K*5 is of the type INTEGER and
C = K*5/J	the results lies outside of the permitted
	range of numbers for INTEGER values. The ter-
	minated "result" is used for further calcu-
	lations without registering an error message.
	The result is incorrect.

<u>Variable D:</u>	To begin with the expression 5/J is cal-
D = K*(5/J)	culated and has the type INTEGER and value 0 .
	The variable D thus receives the value 0.0.

<u>Variable N:</u>

N = (K+0.)*5/J

The expression K+0. is of the type REAL and is identical with the first 6-7 digits of the value of K (rounding errors). The additional intermediate results are also of the type REAL and, apart from rounding errors, the result agrees with the expected value of K/2. In order to show the rounding errors, the FORMAT statement was changed using I11. The details will be described later in chapter 5.

<u>Example 3.1 (page 16)</u>

```
C  EXAMPLE 3.1
      REAL X,Y
      X = -1.
    1 Y = 2.0*X**2+3.0*X-1.
      WRITE (*,100) X,Y
  100 FORMAT (1X,5F15.6)
      X = X+0.1
      IF (X .LE. 1.55) GO TO 1
      STOP
      END
```

The final value was increased by 0.05 in order to calculate the value of the polynomial y for the upper limit 1.5. This is done in order to prevent the possibility that the program does not evaluate the upper limit value due to rounding errors. The following table was printed:

```
    -1.000000      -2.000000
     -.900000      -2.080000
     -.800000      -2.120000
     -.700000      -2.119999
```

```
      .900001       3.320002
     1.000000       4.000000
     1.099999       4.719995
     1.199999       5.479990
     1.299998       6.279984
     1.399998       7.119980
     1.499997       7.999974
```

If the results of the calculation are not output on the printer but rather on a monitor, then the user notices the following: Before the first values have been read and interpreted, all the lines on the monitor are filled and the values to be calculated first are overwritten by succeeding values. In order to prevent this, Fortran 77 is provided with the PAUSE statement. It has the general form:

```
         PAUSE
or       PAUSE 99999
or       PAUSE 'Sequence of characters'
```

The number 99999 represents a sequence of up to 5 digits. The
digits or sequence of characters are output at the terminal
when the PAUSE statement is encountered during program
execution. The program then waits for a response from the console (in general, the "return" key has to be pressed) and then
executes the remaining statements.

In order to illustrate the application, Example 3.1 will be
modified so that up to 20 lines can be output at a time on the
display before the program execution is interrupted by the
PAUSE statement. [*)]

```
      C  EXAMPLE 3.1, SOLUTION FOR SCREEN
            REAL X,Y
            INTEGER N
            X = -1.
          1 N = 0
          2 Y = 2.0*X**2+3.0*X-1.
            WRITE (*,100) X,Y
        100 FORMAT (1X,5F15.6)
            X = X+0.1
            N = N+1
            IF (X .GT. 1.55) STOP
            IF (N .LT. 20) GO TO 2
            PAUSE 'PROGRAM INTERRUPTION'
            GO TO 1
            END
```

If the program is executed in batch operation instead of inter-
actively, then the PAUSE statement has the effect of informing
the console operator of the computer. The program waits for the
response of the operator and, as a result, occupies valuable
computer capacity. The PAUSE statement should, therefore, not
be used in batch operation.

[*)] Some small computers provide for the following possibility:
By pressing the keys CNTL and S at the same time the output is
stopped. The output can only be continued by pressing the keys
CNTL and Q.

<u>Exercise 3.1 (page 25)</u>

<u>Solution a</u>

```
C EXERCISE 3.1, FULL FORTRAN 77
      REAL X,Y
      DO 1 X = -1,1.55,0.1
      Y = 2.*X**2+3.*X-1.
      WRITE (*,100) X,Y
    1 CONTINUE
  100 FORMAT (1X,5F15.6)
      STOP
      END
```

<u>Solution b</u>

The initial value a, the final value e and the increment i are
only allowed to be variables or constants of the type INTEGER
in Fortran 77 subset. Furthermore, the DO-variable has to be
an integer variable. To fulfill these requirements, the program
could have been written as follows:

```
C EXERCISE 3.1, SUBSET
      REAL X,Y
      INTEGER NX
      DO 1 NX = -10, 15, 1
      X = NX/10.
      Y = 2.*X**2+3.*X-1.
      WRITE (*,100) X,Y
    1 CONTINUE
  100 FORMAT (1X,5F15.6)
      STOP
      END
```

The program calculates the same values as in Example 3.1.

<u>Exercise 3.2 (page 26)</u>

```
C EXERCISE 3.2
      REAL X,F,F1
      INTEGER K
      X = 3.
      F = X**2-3.
      F1 = 2*X
      WRITE (*,100) X,F,F1
  100 FORMAT (1X,5F15.6)
      DO 1 K=1,10,1
      X = X-F/F1
      F = X**2-3.
      IF (F .LT. 1E-6 .AND. -F .LT. 1E-6) GO TO 2
      F1 = 2*X
      WRITE (*,100) X,F,F1
    1 CONTINUE
      X = 9999
      F = 9999
    2 WRITE (*,100) X,F
      STOP
      END
```

In order to calculate an approximate value x_{j+1} using the Newton iteration method, only the previous value x_j is required. It is, therefore, only necessary to reserve a single storage place for the various approximate values x_j which are calculated one after the other.

If the iteration does not converge and the desired zero position is not found within ten steps, then the variables X and Y are assigned the value 9999. This acts as a safety device against misinterpretation (the output of texts will be explained later, cf. page 45).

x	f(x)	f'(x)
3.000000	6.000000	6.000000
2.000000	1.000000	4.000000
1.750000	.062500	3.500000
1.732142	.000317	3.464285
1.732051	.000000	

Example 4.1 (page 28)

```
C  EXAMPLE 4.1, FULL FORTRAN 77        C  EXAMPLE 4.1, SUBSET
   REAL X,A(0:2),Y                        REAL X,A(3),Y
   INTEGER K,N                            INTEGER K,N,N1
   N = 2                                  N = 2
   A(0) = -1                              A(1) = -1
   A(1) =  3                              A(2) =  3
   A(2) =  2                              A(3) =  2
   DO 2 X = -1, 1.55, 0.1                 X = -1
   Y = 0                                2 Y = 0
   DO 1 K = N, 0, -1                      N1 = N+1          ] index
   Y = Y*X+A(K)                           DO 1 K = N1, 1, -1] shift
 1 CONTINUE                               Y = Y*X+A(K)
   WRITE (*,100) X,Y                    1 CONTINUE          ]
 2 CONTINUE                              WRITE (*,100) X,Y
100 FORMAT (1X,5F15.6)                    X = X+0.1
   STOP                                   IF (X .LE. 1.55) GO TO 2
   END                                100 FORMAT (1X,5F15.6)
                                          STOP
                                          END
```

Both of the programs calculate the same values as in Example 3.1 (cf. page 112).

Exercise 4.1 (page 36)

```
C  EXERCISE 4.1, FULL FORTRAN 77       C  EXERCISE 4.1, SUBSET
   PARAMETER (N=3)                        REAL A(3,3),B(3),X(3),H
   REAL A(N,N),B(N),X(N),H               INTEGER J,J1,K,K1,M,N,N1
   INTEGER J,K,M                         N = 3
   A(1,1) = 1.0                          A(1,1) = 1.0
   A(1,2) = 0.5                          A(1,2) = 0.5
   A(1,3) = 0.3                          A(1,3) = 0.3
```

<table>
<tr><td>

Full Fortran 77

```
      A(2,1) = 0.2
      A(2,2) = 2.0
      A(2,3) = 0.4
      A(3,1) = 0.2
      A(3,2) = 0.2
      A(3,3) = 1.0
      B(1) = 1.0
      B(2) = 2.0
      B(3) = 3.0

      DO 3 K = 1,N-1,1

      DO 2 J = K+1,N,1
      H = A(J,K)/A(K,K)
      B(J) = B(J)-H*B(K)
      DO 1 M = K+1,N,1
      A(J,M) = A(J,M)-H*A(K,M)
    1 CONTINUE
    2 CONTINUE
    3 CONTINUE
      DO 5 J = N,1,-1

      DO 4 K = N,J+1,-1
      B(J) = B(J)-A(J,K)*X(K)
    4 CONTINUE
      X(J) = B(J)/A(J,J)
    5 CONTINUE
      DO 6 J = 1,N,1
      WRITE (*,100) X(J)
  100 FORMAT (1X,5F15.6)
    6 CONTINUE
      STOP
      END
```

</td><td>

Fortran 77 Subset

```
      A(2,1) = 0.2
      A(2,2) = 2.0
      A(2,3) = 0.4
      A(3,1) = 0.2
      A(3,2) = 0.2
      A(3,3) = 1.0
      B(1) = 1.0
      B(2) = 2.0
      B(3) = 3.0
      N1 = N-1
      DO 3 K = 1,N1,1
      K1 = K+1
      DO 2 J = K1,N,1
      H = A(J,K)/A(K,K)
      B(J) = B(J)-H*B(K)
      DO 1 M = K1,N,1
      A(J,M) = A(J,M)-H*A(K,M)
    1 CONTINUE
    2 CONTINUE
    3 CONTINUE
      DO 5 J = N,1,-1
      J1 = J+1
      DO 4 K = N,J1,-1
      B(J) = B(J)-A(J,K)*X(K)
    4 CONTINUE
      X(J) = B(J)/A(J,J)
    5 CONTINUE
      DO 6 J = 1,N,1
      WRITE (*,100) X(J)
  100 FORMAT (1X,5F15.6)
    6 CONTINUE
      STOP
      END
```

</td></tr>
</table>

The two programs provide the following results

```
      -.091324
       .422374
      2.933788
```

Exercise 4.2 (page 37)

In the program that follows, a new form of output statement will be used, namely:

```
      WRITE(*,100)    (X(I),I=1,N,1),MAX
```

The purpose of this statement is to output the components $x_1,\dots,x_n$ of the vector X (in a single line) using a single statement. This output form ("implied DO-loop") will be considered in detail in Chapter 5.

```fortran
C  EXERCISE 4.2
      REAL C(3,3),D(3),X(3),H,MAX,ABS
      INTEGER J,K,N,NR
      N = 3
      C(1,1) =  0
      C(1,2) = -0.5
      C(1,3) = -0.3
      C(2,1) = -0.1
      C(2,2) =  0
      C(2,3) = -0.2
      C(3,1) = -0.2
      C(3,2) = -0.2
      C(3,3) =  0
      D(1) = 1
      D(2) = 1
      D(3) = 3
      DO 1 J = 1,N,1
      X(J) = 0
    1 CONTINUE
      DO 8888 NR = 1,20,1
      MAX = 0
      DO 3 J = 1,N,1
      H = 0
      DO 2 K = 1,N,1
      H = H+C(J,K)*X(K)
    2 CONTINUE
      H = H+D(J)
      ABS = H-X(J)
      IF (ABS .LT. 0) ABS = -ABS
      IF (ABS .GT. MAX) MAX = ABS
      X(J) = H
    3 CONTINUE
      WRITE (*,100) (X(J),J=1,N,1),MAX
  100 FORMAT (1X,5F15.6)
      IF (MAX .LT. 0.0000005) GO TO 9999
 8888 CONTINUE
      DO 4 J = 1,N,1
      X(J) = 9999
    4 CONTINUE
 9999 DO 5 J = 1,N,1
      WRITE (*,100) X(J)
    5 CONTINUE
      STOP
      END
```

Annotations (right margin):
- DO 1 J = 1,N,1 / X(J) = 0 / 1 CONTINUE ← definition of starting vector
- DO 8888 NR = 1,20,1 ← limitation to 20 iterations
- WRITE (*,100) (X(J),J=1,N,1),MAX ← output of the vector components in a form which will be later described

x_1	x_2	x_3	error
1.000000	.900000	2.620000	2.620000
-.235999	.499600	2.947279	1.235999
-.133984	.423943	2.942008	.102016
-.094573	.421056	2.934703	.039411
-.090939	.422153	2.933757	.003634
-.091204	.422369	2.933766	.000265
-.091314	.422378	2.933786	.000111
-.091325	.422375	2.933789	.000010
-.091324	.422375	2.933789	.000001
-.091324	.422375	2.933789	.000000

-.091324
.422375 ← solution vector
2.933789

<u>Exercise 5.1 (page 49)</u>

```
        C EXERCISE 5.1, FULL FORTRAN 77
              INTEGER A,B,C,D,AB,CD,AC,BD,ABCD
              A = 28
              B = 61
              C = 19
              D = 72
              AB = A+B
              CD = C+D
              AC = A+C
              BD = B+D
              ABCD = AB+CD
              WRITE (*,100)
              WRITE (*,101) A,B,AB
              WRITE (*,102)  C,D,CD
              WRITE (*,103) AC,BD,ABCD
              STOP
          100 FORMAT (T25,'I   +   -  I'/T23,'--+',9('-'),'+----')
          101 FORMAT (T23,'B I',2I4,' I',I4/T25,'I',9X,'I')
          102 FORMAT (T23,'G I',2I4,' I',I4/T23,'--+',9('-'),'+----')
          103 FORMAT (T25,'I',2I4,' I',I4)
              END
```

```
              I   +   -  I
             --+---------+----
             B I  28  61 I  89
             I            I
             G I  19  72 I  91
             --+---------+----
             I   47 133 I 180
```

The tabulator codes T,TL,TR are not defined for the subset
version. Thus, in the above solution, (a-1)X has to replace Ta
in order for the characters to be printed from the column a
onwards:

```
          100 FORMAT (24X,'I   +   -  I'/22X,'--+',9('-'),'+----')
          101 FORMAT (22X,'B I',2I4,' I',I4/24X,'I',9X,'I')
          102 FORMAT (22X,'G I',2I4,' I',I4/22X,'--+',9('-'),'+----')
          103 FORMAT (24X,'I',2I4,' I',I4)
              END
```

<u>Exercise 5.2 (page 51)</u>

```
        C EXERCISE 5.2
              REAL A(3,2)
              INTEGER J,K
              DO 2 J = 1,3,1
              DO 1 K = 1,2,1
              A(J,K) = J+K/10.0
            1 CONTINUE
            2 CONTINUE
              WRITE (*, 100) A
```

```
      DO 3 J = 1,3,1
      WRITE (*,100) (A(J,K), K=1,2,1)
    3 CONTINUE
      WRITE (*,100) ((A(J,K), K=1,2,1), J=1,3,1)
  100 FORMAT (2F4.1)
      STOP
      END
```

a)   WRITE (*, 100) A

Output: 1.1 2.1
               3.1 1.2
               2.2 3.2

The elements of matrix A are stored in columns as a vector.
The format results in pairs of values being output in a single
line. Now since the matrix A has three rows, the third value
of the first column vector is printed in the next line and the
first value of the second column vector is printed next to it
etc.. Hence the values that are output do not have the same
order as the matrix A and it is, therefore, not recommended to
use this form of output.

b)   DO 3 J = 1,3,1
        WRITE (*,100) (A(J,K), K=1,2,1)
      3 CONTINUE

Output: 1.1 1.2
               2.1 2.2
               3.1 3.2

Every row of the matrix is output by means of a special WRITE
statement. The matrix form of A can be immediately recognized.

c)   WRITE (*,100) ((A(J,K), K=1,2,1), J=1,3,1)

This statement produces the same print out as b). If, however,
the number of columns of matrix A does not correspond to the
number of the format codes, then the matrix elements are output
(row by row) one after the other which results in the corresponding matrix form not being recognizable. Thus, in general,
it is recommended to use output form b).

Exercise 6.1 (page 57)

a) The variable N is read from the first input line and using
   the format code I2 it receives the value 4. The value of N
   is used immediately by the implied DO-loop

        (A(J),J=0,N,1)

   in the same statement. Thus, five values are read for the
   components $a_0, \ldots, a_4$.
   Due to

        (T5,2F5.1)

   the values 1.8 and 9.6 are transferred to A(0) and A(1) from
   column 5 onwards in the first input line. (Columns 3 and 4
   containing the digits 6,7 are ignored). Since the format,
   not however the input list, has been processed, the values
   -0.3 and 0 (the value 0 is assumed by the computer as no
   number appears in the second field) of the second input line
   are transferred to the components A(2) and A(3). In order to
   do this, the following format was used:

        (T5,2F5.1)

   The final input line provides the number 1.0 for component
   A(4) using the same format statement. Since the input has
   now been completed, the last number (4.5) is ignored.

b) With respect to the program segment described, the limitations
   of the subset version of Fortran 77 result in the following
   difficulties:
   - The lower limit of the index of a field is always 1 .
   - It is not possible to use a tabulator in the format state-
     ment.

   If the input data is presented in the same manner, then the
   program has to be modified as follows:

```
      INTEGER J,N
      REAL A(11)
      READ (*,100) N,(A(J+1), J=0,N,1)
  100 FORMAT (I2,2X,2F5.1/(4X,2F5.1))
      ...
```

Exercise 6.2 (page 58)

```
     C  EXERCISE 6.2
           REAL X,M
           INTEGER N
           N = 0
           M = 0
           WRITE (*,111)
       111 FORMAT (' INPUT OF VALUES, FORMAT: F5.1, ,
         *           ' AT END INPUT OF: CR AND ETX ')
      1111 READ (*,100,END=9999) X
       100 FORMAT (F5.1)
           N = N+1
           M = M+X
           GO TO 1111
      9999 M = M/N
           WRITE (*,101) N,M
       101 FORMAT (' N =',I3,'   MEAN VALUE =',F8.2)
           STOP
           END
```

> Input of the values 1,2,...,5

```
     N =  5  MEAN VALUE =    3.00
```

The "infinite" loop which is formed by means of

```
     1111 READ (...,END=...) ...
          ...
          GOTO 1111
```

can only be left by means of the END condition. Only after all
data has been read will branching to statement number 9999 take
place because of END = 9999. The mean value is determinated
here and printed together with the number of the input values
(= the number of input lines). Finally the program is terminated by means of the STOP statement. If it has been overlooked
to input data, then the program is interrupted at line

```
     9999 M=M/N
```

with an error message (division by zero due to N=0).

Exercise 7.1 (page 66)

The variable LINE has been declared to have a length of 1, and
as a result only the first character of the CHARACTER constant
'HEADLINE' is transferred, (i.e. LINE = 'H').
Finally the WRITE statement results in the following line
being printed:

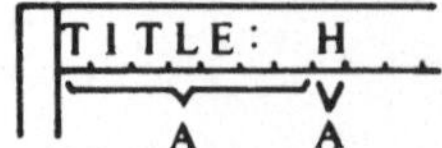

The READ statement and the format codes A2 and A6 result in
the letters XY and JKLMNO respectively being read. The following are stored in the variables:

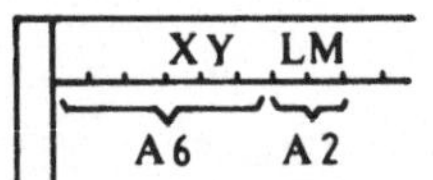

The characters JK to the left are ignored.

As a result of the following output statement, the line below
is printed

The characters to the right NO belonging
to the variable C are omitted.

Exercise 7.2 (page 66)

```
C  EXERCISE 7.2
       CHARACTER*20 IN,INDEX(100)
       INTEGER NMAX,POINTER,J
       NMAX = 1
       WRITE (*,111)
   111 FORMAT (' NOW INPUT OF THE WORDS, CLOSE WITH CR AND ETX')
       READ (*,100) INDEX(1)
  1111 READ (*,100,END=9999) IN
   100 FORMAT (A)
       DO 1 POINTER = 1,NMAX,1
       IF (IN .LT. INDEX(POINTER)) GO TO 22
     1 CONTINUE
       POINTER = NMAX+1
    22 NMAX = NMAX+1
       DO 2 J = NMAX,POINTER+1,-1
       INDEX(J) = INDEX(J-1)
     2 CONTINUE
       INDEX(POINTER) = IN
       GO TO 1111
  9999 DO 3 J = 1,NMAX,1
       WRITE (*,101) INDEX(J)
   101 FORMAT (1X,A20)
     3 CONTINUE
       STOP
       END
```

FORMAT		BIT	
BIT		CHARACTER	
INTEGER	input	EXERCISE	output
EXERCISE		FORMAT	
CHARACTER		INTEGER	
REAL		REAL	

Example 7.1 (page 69)

```
      C EXAMPLE 7.1, FULL FORTRAN 77
            CHARACTER C(0:50),BLANK,ASTER
            REAL X,Y,VAL(100,2),YMIN,YMAX,H
            INTEGER K,L,J,JMAX
            DATA BLANK,C,ASTER /52*' ','*'/,YMIN,YMAX /0.0,0.0/
            JMAX = 0
            DO 1 X = -1,1.01,0.05
            JMAX = JMAX+1
            VAL(JMAX,1) = X
            Y = 16*X**5-20*X**3+5*X
            VAL(JMAX,2) = Y
            IF (Y .GT. YMAX) YMAX = Y
            IF (Y .LT. YMIN) YMIN = Y
          1 CONTINUE
            H = 50/(YMAX-YMIN)
            DO 2 J = 1,JMAX,1
            L = H*(VAL(J,2)-YMIN)
            C(L) = ASTER
            WRITE (*,100) VAL(J,1),VAL(J,2),(C(K), K=0,L,1)
        100 FORMAT (1X,F6.2,F8.3,2X,51A1)
            C(L) = BLANK
          2 CONTINUE
            STOP
            END
      -1.00  -1.000  *
       -.95    .017
       -.90    .632
       -.85    .933
       -.80    .997
       -.75    .891
```

Example 8.1 (page 72)

```
      C EXAMPLE 8.1, WITH STATEMENT FUNCTION
            CHARACTER C(0:50),BLANK,ASTER
            REAL X,Y,VAL(100,2),YMIN,YMAX,H,X1,FCT
            INTEGER K,L,J,JMAX
            DATA BLANK,C,ASTER /52*' ','*'/,
           *      YMIN,YMAX /0.0,0.0/
            FCT(X1) = 16*X1**5-20*X1**3+5*X1
            JMAX = 0
            DO 1 X = -1,1.01,0.05
            JMAX = JMAX+1
            VAL(JMAX,1) = X
            Y = FCT(X)
            VAL(JMAX,2) = Y
            IF (Y .GT. YMAX) YMAX = Y
            IF (Y .LT. YMIN) YMIN = Y
          1 CONTINUE
            H = 50/(YMAX-YMIN)
            DO 2 J = 1,JMAX,1
            L = H*(VAL(J,2)-YMIN)
            C(L) = ASTER
            WRITE (*,100) VAL(J,1),VAL(J,2),(C(K), K=0,L,1)
        100 FORMAT (1X,F6.2,F8.3,2X,51A1)
            C(L) = BLANK
          2 CONTINUE
            STOP
            END
```

124

<u>Example 8.2 (page 75)</u>

```
C  EXAMPLE 8.2, FULL FORTRAN 77
      REAL X,Y,A(0:5)
      INTEGER J
      DATA (A(J), J=0,5,1) /0., 5., 0., -20., 0., 16./
      DO 1 X = -1,1.05,0.1
      WRITE (*,100) X,Y(X,A,5)
  100 FORMAT (1X,F6.2,F8.3)
    1 CONTINUE
      STOP
      END
```
        main program

```
      REAL FUNCTION Y(X1,A1,N1)
      REAL X1,A1(0:N1),S
      INTEGER N1,J
      S = 0
      DO 1 J = N1,0,-1
      S = S*X1+A1(J)
    1 CONTINUE
      Y = S
      RETURN
      END
```
        function subprogram
             y

<u>Hint:</u> For a correct transfer of the vector A as an actual para-
meter to the subprogram Y, it is important that the lower
index limit 0 is declared for the formal parameter A1 in
the declaration phase of the subprogram.

```
C  EXAMPLE 8.2, SUBSET
      REAL X,Y,A(6),YV
      INTEGER J
      DATA A /0., 5., 0., -20., 0., 16./
      X = -1
    1 YV = Y(X,A,5)
      WRITE (*,100) X,YV
  100 FORMAT (1X,F6.2,F8.3)
      X = X+0.1
      IF (X .LE. 1.05) GO TO 1
      STOP
      END

      REAL FUNCTION Y(X1,A1,N1)
      REAL X1,A1(1),S
      INTEGER N1,J,J1
      S = 0
      J1 = N1+1
      DO 1 J = J1,0,-1
      S = S*X1+A1(J)
    1 CONTINUE
      Y = S
      RETURN
      END
```

```
-1.00    1.000
 -.90    -.569
 -.80    -.798
    〜
  .80    -.798
  .90    -.569
 1.00    1.000
```
        output of the
        results is the
        same for both programs

Example 8.3 (page 77)

The integration interval [0, 1] was chosen for the running of
the program. The approximate value of 1.00 which was determined
for the integral value (=1-1/6) lies within the estimated error
(cf. the hint given with Exercise 8.1 on the next page).

```
      C EXAMPLE 8.3
            REAL A,B,TRAP,F,V
            EXTERNAL F
            A = 0
            B = 1
            V = TRAP(A,B,F)
            WRITE (*,100) V
        100 FORMAT (1X,F6.2)
            STOP
            END

            REAL FUNCTION F(X)
            REAL X
            F = X**2-X+1
            RETURN
            END

            REAL FUNCTION TRAP(X1,X2,FCT)
            REAL X1,X2,FCT
            TRAP = (FCT(X1)+FCT(X2))*(X2-X1)/2
            RETURN
            END

        1.00       ◄──────────────── result
```

Exercise 8.1 (page 78)

1) To begin with, care has to be taken in choosing the number
   of partial intervals in order for the error to be within
   the acceptable range.
   The integration error R_i can be estimated for each partial
   interval T_i and length $h = \dfrac{b-a}{n}$

$$|R_i| < \frac{h^3}{12} \max_{T_i} |f''(x)|$$

The following applies for the total integration error:

$$|R| < \sum_i |R_i| < \frac{h^3}{12} \max_{[a,b]} |f''(x)| \sum_i 1$$

$$< \frac{(b-a)^3}{12 \cdot n^2} \max_{[a,b]} |f''(x)|$$

The second derivative is given by

$$f''(x) = 40 \cdot (8x^3 - 3x)$$

and this gives the estimation

$$\max |f''(x)| \leqslant 200$$

Since the integration error should be not greater than 10^{-6}, the rough estimation

$$\frac{2^3}{12\, n^2}\ 200 \overset{!}{<} 10^{-6}$$

results in $n \geqslant 6000$. Now since 6000 additions can cause the rounding errors to become too high for single precision,[*] double precision has to be used for the items in the program. This means, however, that the problem – in this form – cannot be solved in Fortran 77 subset, since the variable type DOUBLE PRECISION is not provided for.

2) On the other hand, the integral can easily be solved "by hand" since

$$\int_{-1}^{1} f(x)\,dx = \frac{16}{6}x^6 - \frac{20}{4}x^4 + \frac{5}{2}x^2 \Big|_{-1}^{1} = 0$$

This illustrates the following: It is worth, also in other cases, to take into account the symmetry properties of functions in order to reduce the computing time or even do away it completely (see above). It is also worth carrying out a more exact error estimation, since this provides a possibility to reduce the number of intervals.

```
C  EXERCISE 8.1
       DOUBLE PRECISION INTEGR,F,TRAP
       INTEGER N
       EXTERNAL F
       N = 6000
       INTEGR = TRAP(-1D0, 1D0, F, N)
       WRITE (*,100) N,INTEGR
  100 FORMAT (1X,I6,F20.15)
       STOP
       END
```

main program

[*] Using simple precision of 6-7 digits, cf. Appendix A, page 133.

```fortran
      DOUBLE PRECISION FUNCTION F(X)
      DOUBLE PRECISION X
      F = 16*X**5-20*X**3+5*X
      RETURN
      END

      DOUBLE PRECISION FUNCTION TRAP(A,B,FCT,N)
      DOUBLE PRECISION A,B,FCT,S,H,X
      INTEGER N
      H = (B-A)/N
      S = (FCT(A)+FCT(B))/2
      DO 1 X = A+H, B-H*0.5, H
      S = S+FCT(X)
    1 CONTINUE
      TRAP = S*H
      RETURN
      END
```

The bracketed annotations read: *function subprogram F* and *function subprogram TRAP*.

```
 6000   -.000000000000018
```

This line is annotated: *output of N and the integral value INTEGR*.

Exercise 9.1 (page 81)

Appropriate output statements have been included in subroutine HALVE in order to illustrate the alternate calculations at the two interval limits.

```fortran
C EXERCISE 9.1
      INTEGER N
      REAL A,B,F,XZERO
      EXTERNAL F
      A = 0
      B = 1.570796
      CALL HALVE(A,B,F,XZERO,N)
      IF (N .EQ. 0) WRITE (*,100) XZERO
  100 FORMAT (1X,F10.6)
      STOP
      END

      REAL FUNCTION F(X)
      REAL X
      F = SIN(X)-0.2
      RETURN
      END

      SUBROUTINE HALVE(A,B,FCT,X,N)
      REAL A,B,FCT,X,X1,X2,Y,Y1,Y2
      INTEGER N
      N = -1
      Y1 = FCT(A)
      WRITE (*,100) A,Y1
      Y2 = FCT(B)
      WRITE (*,101) B,Y2
      X1 = A
      X2 = B
```

```
          IF (Y1*Y2 .GT. 0) THEN
            WRITE (*,102)
            RETURN
          ELSE
   1111    X = (X1+X2)*0.5
           Y = FCT(X)
           IF (ABS(Y) .LT. 1.E-5) THEN
             N = 0
             RETURN
           ELSE
             IF (Y*Y1 .GT. 0 ) THEN
               X1 = X
               WRITE (*,100) X1,Y
               GO TO 1111
             ELSE
               X2 = X
               WRITE (*,101) X2,Y
               GO TO 1111
             END IF
           END IF
          END IF
     100 FORMAT ( 1X,2F10.6)
     101 FORMAT (23X,2F10.6)
     102 FORMAT (' FUNCTION HAS THE SAME SIGN AT THE POINTS A AND B')
         END
```

It is not necessary to store the function values (Y1=Y and Y2=Y) since it is only the signs of Y1 and Y2 that are important.

values at the left limit		values at the right limit	
.000000	-.200000		
		1.570796	.800000
		.785398	.507107
		.392699	.182683
.196350	-.004910		
		.201718	.000353
.201335	-.000023		
		.201527	.000165
		.201431	.000071
		.201383	.000024
.201359			

Exercise 9.2 (page 85)

The exercise requires that the given equation system should not be changed by the subprogram. In addition it requires that the auxiliary fields A1 and B1 have to be declared in subroutine GAUSS and that the initial fields have to be stored in these auxiliary fields.

In doing so, the index limits of the auxiliary fields have to be defined using constants since Fortran does not provide for a "dynamic field declaration". The definition of the index limits does, of course, greatly restrict the possible applications of the subroutine. Therefore, in practice it is allowed to change those fields which are transferred to the subprogram.

```fortran
C  EXERCISE 9.2
      REAL A(20,20),B(20),X(20)
      INTEGER N,J,K
      LOGICAL SOL
      READ (*,100) N
      WRITE (*,100) N
  100 FORMAT (I5)
      DO 1 J = 1,N,1
      READ  (*,101) (A(J,K), K=1,N,1), B(J)
      WRITE (*,101) (A(J,K), K=1,N,1), B(J)
  101 FORMAT (8F10.3)
    1 CONTINUE
      CALL GAUSS(N,A,B,X,SOL)
      IF (.NOT. SOL) STOP
      WRITE (*,102) (X(J), J=1,N,1)
  102 FORMAT (' THE SOLUTION VECTOR HAS THE COMPONENTS:'//
     *         7(F10.5,2X))
      STOP
      END

      SUBROUTINE GAUSS(N,A,B,X,S)
      REAL A(20,20),B(20),X(20),A1(20,20),B1(20),H
      LOGICAL S
      INTEGER J,J1,J2,JH,K,N
      DO 2 J = 1,N,1
      DO 1 K = 1,N,1
      A1(J,K) = A(J,K)
    1 CONTINUE
      B1(J) = B(J)
    2 CONTINUE
      DO 8888 J = 1,N,1
      J1 = J
      H = ABS(A1(J,J))
      JH = J+1
      DO 3 J2 = JH,N,1
      IF (ABS(A1(J2,J)) .LE. H) GO TO 3
      H = ABS(A1(J2,J))
      J1 = J2
    3 CONTINUE
      IF (H .GT. 1.E-5) GO TO 4
      S = .FALSE.
      WRITE (*,100)
  100 FORMAT (' MATRIX IS SINGULAR')
      RETURN
    4 DO 5 K = J,N,1
      H = A1(J,K)
      A1(J,K) = A1(J1,K)
      A1(J1,K) = H
    5 CONTINUE
      H = B1(J)
      B1(J) = B1(J1)
      B1(J1) = H
      H = 1/A1(J,J)
      DO 6 K = J,N,1
      A1(J,K) = A1(J,K)*H
    6 CONTINUE
```

```
        B1( J) = B1( J)*H
        JH = J+1
        DO 8 J2 = JH, N, 1
        DO 7 K = JH, N, 1
        A1( J2, K) = A1( J2, K)-A1( J, K)*A1( J2, J)
      7 CONTINUE
        B1( J2) = B1( J2)-B1( J)*A1( J2, J)
      8 CONTINUE
   8888 CONTINUE
        S = .TRUE.
        DO 10 J = N, 1, -1
        X( J) = B1( J)
        JH = J+1
        DO 9 K = N, JH, -1
        X( J) = X( J)-A1( J, K)*X( K)
      9 CONTINUE
     10 CONTINUE
        RETURN
        END
      3
        .200        .200      1.000      3.000
       1.000        .500       .300      1.000
        .200       2.000       .400      2.000
   THE SOLUTION VECTOR HAS THE COMPONENTS:

        .09132       .42237      2.93379
```

<u>Exercise 12.1 (page 105)</u>

The program is extended by several output statements for the print out in order to make the "sorting by means of insertion" easier to understand. Only the sorting key was printed. Using appropriate control statements, the logical units 1 and 2 were assigned to the existing files MO7A.DAT1 and MO7A.DAT2. For output, the file to be newly created MO7A.DAT3 was assigned to the logical unit 3.

```
      C  EXERCISE 12.1
         INTEGER N1, N2
         LOGICAL E1, E2, SH
         CHARACTER*40 T1, T2
         DATA E1, E2, SH /3*.FALSE./
         OPEN( 1, FILE=' FILE1')
         OPEN( 2, FILE=' FILE2')
         OPEN( 3, FILE=' FILE3')
   1111 READ ( 1, 100, END=4444) N1, T1
         WRITE ( *, 101) N1
         IF ( SH) GO TO 3333
         SH = .TRUE.
   2222 READ ( 2, 100, END=5555) N2, T2
         WRITE ( *, 102) N2
```

```
3333 IF (E1) THEN
        WRITE (3,100) N2,T2
        WRITE (*,103) N2
        GO TO 2222
     END IF
     IF (E2) THEN
        WRITE (3,100) N1,T1
        WRITE (*,103) N1
        GO TO 1111
     END IF
     IF (N1 .LT. N2) THEN
        WRITE (3,100) N1,T1
        WRITE (*,103) N1
        GO TO 1111
     ELSE
        WRITE (3,100) N2,T2
        WRITE (*,103) N2
        GO TO 2222
     END IF
4444 E1 = .TRUE.
     IF (E2) GO TO 9999
     GO TO 3333
5555 E2 = .TRUE.
     IF (.NOT. E1) GO TO 3333
9999 CLOSE(1)
     CLOSE(2)
     CLOSE(3)
     STOP
 100 FORMAT (I5,A40)
 101 FORMAT ( 1X,I5)
 102 FORMAT (10X,I5)
 103 FORMAT ( 5X,I5)
     END
```

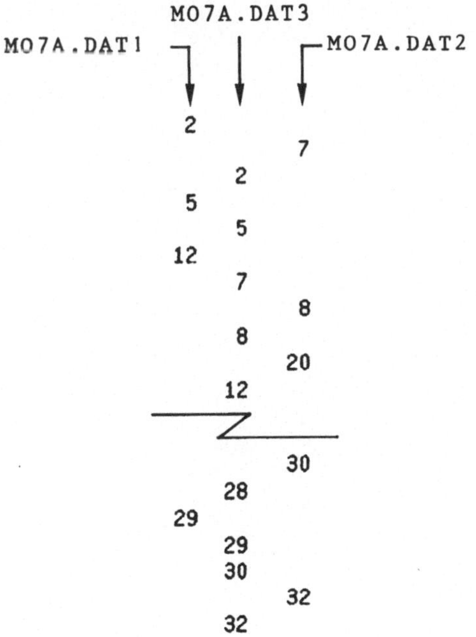

```
                  MO7A.DAT3
MO7A.DAT1       ┐      │    ┌─MO7A.DAT2
                ▼      ▼    ▼
                2
                       7
                   2
                5
                   5
               12
                   7
                       8
                   8
                       20
                12
              ────────┐
                      └─────
                       30
                   28
              29
                   29
                   30
                       32
                   32
```

<u>Exercise 12.2 (page 107)</u>

In the following suggested solution, the two files were organized as direct access files. By storing the record addresses
(N1 and N2) in each other's files, it is implied that it is not
necessary to store both files in a synchronous manner.

```
      C  EXERCISE 12.2
            INTEGER N,N1,N2,NMAX
            REAL SAL,DED
            CHARACTER*20 NAME,ADDR
            OPEN(1,ACCESS='DIRECT',FORM='FORMATTED',RECL=45)
            OPEN(2,ACCESS='DIRECT',FORM='FORMATTED',RECL=45)
            N = 2
            READ (2,100,REC=1) NMAX
      1111 IF (N .GT. NMAX) STOP
            READ (2,100,REC=N) N1,SAL,DED
       100 FORMAT (I5,2F10.2)
            READ (1,101,REC=N1) N2,NAME,ADDR
       101 FORMAT (I5,2A20)
            WRITE (*,102) NAME,ADDR,SAL,DED
       102 FORMAT (1X,A20/1X,A20/1X,2F10.2/)
            N = N+1
            GO TO 1111
            END


         A. B. SMITH
         WESTBORO, MA 00135
           2475.50     241.65

         D. M. NEWTON
         SOUTHBORO MA 00274
            567.44      32.10
```

Appendix A: **Internal Representation of Numbers**

Internal Representation of Numbers

The internal representation of numbers (type INTEGER or REAL)
depends on the computer. As a result, only the storage principle and the consequences arising from it will be described
here. For more detailed information one should consult the
corresponding computer manuals.

I. Integer Numbers (type INTEGER)

Every integer number can be represented by a binary number,
e.g.

$$59_{decimal} = \underline{1} \cdot 2^5 + \underline{1} \cdot 2^4 + \underline{1} \cdot 2^3 + \underline{0} \cdot 2^2 + \underline{1} \cdot 2^1 + \underline{1} \cdot 2^0$$

$$= 111011_{binary}$$

The sequence of digits of the binary number is stored in a
right-aligned manner in the word:

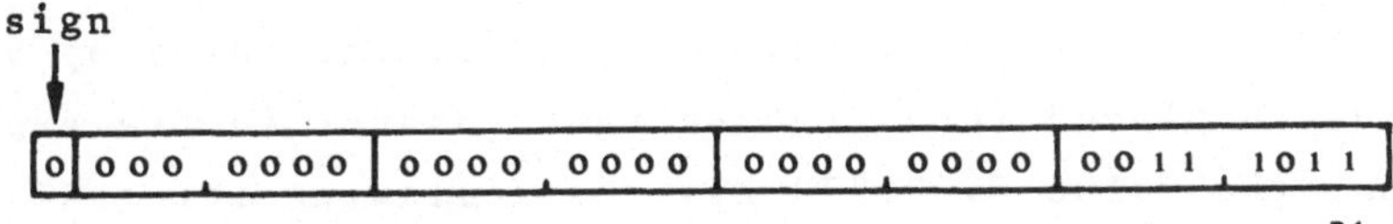

bit position: 0   31

Since the bit position 0 is used for the encoding of the sign,
it is possible to store integer numbers

$$\text{from } -2^{31} \text{ to } 2^{31}-1$$

in one word (= a storage place) (2^{31} = 2 147 483 648 ~ $2 \cdot 10^9$).
Small computers usually only have 16 bits, and not 32 bits,
available for the encoding of INTEGER values. Hence integer
numbers from -2^{15} to $2^{15}-1$ can be encoded in a single storage
place (2^{15} = 32768).

II. Normalized Numbers (type REAL)

Every number z, which is not equal to zero, can be normalized
in the form:

$$z = b \cdot 10^e \quad \text{mit} \quad \frac{1}{10} \leqslant |b| < 1$$

Example

$$0.001273 = 0.1273 \cdot 10^{-2}$$

Computers normalize using the base 16 instead of the base 10: [*]

Hence the following applies:

$$z = b \cdot 16^e \qquad\qquad \frac{1}{16} \leqslant |b| < 1$$

For example, we obtain

$$0.001273_{dec} = 0.00536D65\ldots_{hex} \sim 0.536D65_{hex} \cdot 16^{-2}$$

The word used to store a number is divided into fixed fields

- for the sign
- for the exponent e and
- for the mantissa b

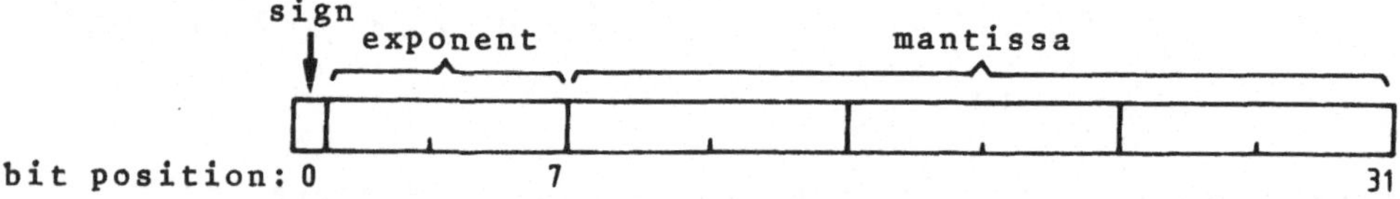

In order to be able to also encode numbers with the negative exponents, the (external) exponent is increased by 64 and this value is placed in a right-aligned manner in the exponent field. Thus, the value 0.001273 has the following internal represen-tation:

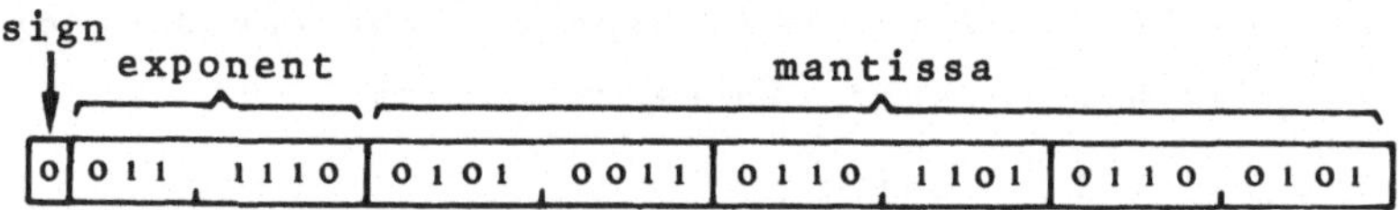

If it is required to form a hexadecimal digit using 4 binary digits, then the number 0.001273 is encoded in a word as follows:

It is possible to represent numbers whose magnitudes lie be-tween

$$\frac{1}{16} \cdot 16^{-64} \quad \text{and} \quad (1 - 16^{-6}) \cdot 16^{63}$$

These values correspond approximately to

$$0.54 \cdot 10^{-78} \quad \text{and} \quad 7.2 \cdot 10^{75}.$$

---

[*] This also depends on the computer being used; normalization on the basis of 8 and 2 is also common.

The following applies for every normalized number z ($\neq 0$):

$$z = b \cdot 16^e \text{ with } 0.1_{hex} \leqslant |b| \leqslant 0.\text{FFFFFF}_{hex} = 1 - 16^{-6}$$

The difference dz of two neighbouring values is given by

$$dz = 16^{-6} \cdot 16^e,$$

which results in the following estimation:

$$16^{-5} = \frac{16^{-6} \cdot 16^e}{0,1_{hex} \cdot 16^e} \geqslant \left|\frac{dz}{z}\right| \geqslant \frac{16^{-6} \cdot 16^e}{(1-16^{-6}) \cdot 16^e} \sim 16^{-6}$$

for the relative error dz/z.

The relative error lies between 16^{-6} and 16^{-5} which corresponds to values between 10^{-7} and 10^{-6}. The consequences are: The internal number representation of the type REAL in the computer results in only a correct interpretation of numbers up to the sixth or seventh place after the decimal point. It is, therefore, a waste of time to ask the computer to seek for relative errors which are smaller than 10^{-5}.

The type

    DOUBLE PRECISION | not included in the subset

is available for solving problems requiring high accuracy. In doing so, two storage places are combined to form a double word, the first of which has the same structure as variables of the type REAL and the second can be used for recording 8 additional (hexadecimal) digits. We thus have the following situation:

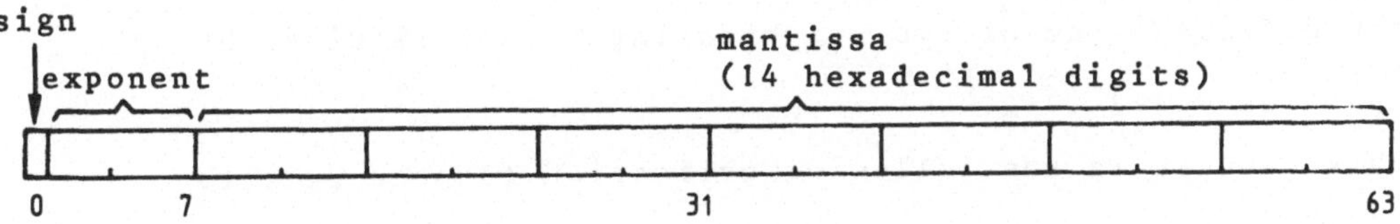

Consideration of the points mentioned above results in a relative error dz/z leading to an error which lies between 16^{-14} and 16^{-13} for double precision representation. Hence when storing a number, this corresponds to 15 to 16 digits being stored correctly after the decimal point. However, for the case of long calculations, even the use of double precision can lead to a loss of accuracy.

Small computers use two 16-bit words for the representation of REAL items. The computer used by us has the following structure:

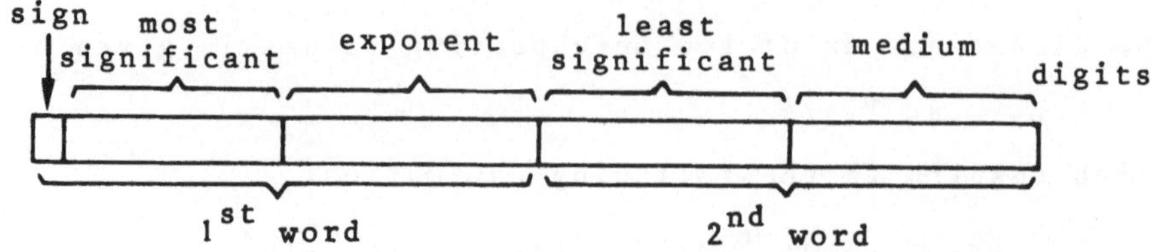

Numbers z that are not equal to zero are normalized as follows:

$$z = b \cdot 2^e \qquad \text{with} \qquad 1 \leqslant |b| < 2$$

The external exponent e is increased by 129 and stored in the exponent field. Since the decimal fraction always has the form 1.dd...d, the value of 0.dd...d is calculated in the binary system and the sequence of digits (without 0.) is encoded as the mantissa b. For the case of negative numbers, the binary complement of the positive number is represented in the first word.

Example:

$$0.001273 = 1.303552 \cdot 2^{-10}$$
$$= (1 + 0.010\ 0110\ 1101\ 1010\ 1100\ 1010_{bin}) \cdot 2^{-10}$$

The difference dz of two neighbouring values is given by

$$dz = 1 \cdot 2^{-23} \cdot 2^e$$

this results in the following estimation for the relative error dz/z:

$$1.2 \cdot 10^{-7} \sim \frac{2^{-23} \cdot 2^e}{1.0 \cdot 2^e} \geqslant \left| \frac{dz}{z} \right| \geqslant \frac{2^{-23} \cdot 2^e}{(2 - 2^{-23}) \cdot 2^e} \sim 0.6 \cdot 10^{-7}$$

The relative error lies between $0.6 \cdot 10^{-7}$ and $1.2 \cdot 10^{-7}$ and is thus smaller than the hexadecimal representation described above. The absolute value of the range of numbers lies between

$$1.5 \cdot 10^{-39} \sim 2^{-129} \leqslant |z| \leqslant 2^{126} \sim 8.5 \cdot 10^{37}.$$

Appendix B: DO-loop

The DO-loop has the following general form: [*]

	Recommended form
DO n d = a,e,i	DO n d = a,e,i
s_1	s_1
...	...
n s_m	s_m
	n CONTINUE

It is allowed to place a comma after the statement number n in the DO-statement in order to separate the number from the DO-variable d which follows. If the increment i is not given, i.e. the form

    DO n d = a,e

is used, then the increment i is assumed to have the value 1 (INTEGER).

All statements from s_1 to s_m belong to the DO-loop. Since the final statement of the loop is not allowed to be one of the following

- GOTO
- arithmetic IF, Block IF, ELSE, END IF
- RETURN, STOP, END
- DO-statement

it is recommended, after the statements $s_1, \ldots s_m$, to label the end of the loop by means of the empty statement

    n CONTINUE

It is obvious that the execution of the loop is terminated if it is left as a result of a skip statement GOTO. This also applies for the statements STOP and RETURN.

The DO-loop is processed in the following manner:

1. The arithmetic expressions a, e and i are evaluated and

---

[*] a) The DO-variable d may be of the type INTEGER, REAL or DOUBLE PRECISION in full Fortran 77. Arithmetic expressions having these types are allowed for a, e, and i.
   b) The DO-variable has to have the type INTEGER in the subset, and a, e, and i are only allowed to be INTEGER constants or variables.

transformed into the type of the DO-variable d. The corresponding values are characterized by w_1, w_e and w_i.

2. a) The DO-variable d is assigned the initial value w_a.

   b) An integer DO-counter c is established and assigned the value

$$c = \max\left(\left[\frac{w_e - w_a + w_i}{w_i} \right], 0 \right)$$

3. It is checked to determine whether the DO-counter c possesses a positive value or the value zero.

   a) If c is positive, then the statements $s_1, \ldots, s_m$ of the loop are executed.
      Finally
       - the DO-variable d is increased by the value w_i (the step length)
       - the DO-counter c is reduced by 1

      and the program branches back to point 3, (i.e. the test of the DO-counter c).

   b) If the DO-counter c is zero, then the program continues with the statement immediately following the loop.

When using DO-loops, attention should be paid to the following points:

 - The value w_i of the increment should not be zero.
 - It is not allowed to assign any values to the items d, a, e and i within the loop.
 - Skips are not allowed from points outside a loop to inside the loop.
 - After leaving a DO-loop (by means of branching to a point outside or after processing the loop), the variables under consideration (DO-variable, and if necessary other variables) possess the values which they were finally assigned.
 - If several DO-loops are nested within each other, then the internal loops have to lie within the others.

Example:

```
     ┌     DO 9 K = 1,20,1
     │     L = K
     │  ┌  DO 8 J = 10,1,1
     │  │  M = J
     │  └ 8 CONTINUE
     └    9 CONTINUE
```

After processing the two loops, the variables possess
the following values: K = 21, L = 20, J = 10. The value
of the variable M is not defined since the internal
loop is not executed.

Example:

```
           ┌     DO 9 K = 1,20,1                      ┌     DO 9 K = 1,20,1
           │     ...                                  │     ...
           │  ┌  DO 8 J = K,20,1                      │  ┌  DO 8 J = K,20,1
Allowed    │  │  ...                  Not allowed     │  │  ...
           │  └ 8 CONTINUE                            │  └ 9 CONTINUE
           │     ...                                  │     ...
           └    9 CONTINUE                            └    8 CONTINUE
```

Hint: Using almost the same syntax, Fortran IV processes
      DO-loops in a different manner: The DO-variable d is
      assigned the initial value a and the statements $s_1, \ldots, s_m$
      are executed. Only after this, it is checked to see if
      the DO-variable d has exceeded the final value e. This
      results in the loop being processed at least once.
      Attention should be paid to this difference when changing
      programs from Fortran IV to Fortran 77.

Appendix C: Supplied Function Subprograms

a) Functions for Type Transformation

Name		Type		Number of Arguments	Call	Meaning
Generic	Specific	Result	Argument			
–	CHAR	ch	I	1	CHAR (n)	the character which is represented by number n
CMPLX	–	C	D, I, C or R	1	CMPLX (a)	$= a + 0 \cdot i$ $(i = \sqrt{-1})$
			D, I or R	2	CMPLX (a, b)	$= a + b \cdot i$ with possible loss of accuracy
DBLE	–	D	D, I, C or R	1	DBLE (a)	1) = a in the possible precision (if a: D, I or R) 2) = Real part of a, if a is complex
–	ICHAR	I	ch	1	ICHAR (c)	= the integer number which represents character c
INT	IFIX, INT **IDINT**	I	R D	1	INT (a)	$\Big\}$ $= \mathrm{sign}\,(a) \cdot [\![a]\!]$
	–		C		INT (z)	as above, whereby a: Real part (z)
	–		I		INT (n)	= n
REAL	FLOAT, REAL **SNGL**		I D	1	REAL (a)	$\Big\}$ = a in single precision
		R	C			= Real part of a
	–		R			= a

The following abbreviations were used here and also in the next table

C	**COMPLEX**
ch	**CHARACTER**
D	**DOUBLE PRECISION**
I	**INTEGER**
L	**LOGICAL**
R	**REAL**

The following characters were used as argument(s)

a, b	items of type	C, D, I or R
c	" " "	ch
n	" " "	I
z	" " "	C

Bold Type: Only defined in full Fortran 77, not in the subset.

b) Mathematical Functions

Name		Type		Number of	Call	Meaning
Generic	Specific	Result	Argument	Arguments		
ABS	**ABS** **CABS** **DABS** IABS	R R D I	R C D I	1	ABS (a)	$= \lvert a \rvert$ $= ((\mathrm{Re}\,(a))^2 + (\mathrm{Im}\,(a))^2)^{1/2}$ $= \lvert a \rvert$ $= \lvert a \rvert$ — in the respective precision
ACOS	**ACOS** DACOS	R D	R D	1	ACOS (a)	inverse functions of cos, sin, tan
ASIN	**ASIN** DASIN	R D	R D	1	ASIN (a)	
ATAN	**ATAN** DATAN	R D	R D	1	ATAN (a)	
ATAN2	ATAN2 DATAN2	R D	R D	2	ATAN2 (a, b)	$= \mathrm{arc\ tan}\left(\frac{a}{b}\right)$
–	**AIMAG**	R	C	1	AIMAG (z)	$= \mathrm{Im}\,(z)$ (Imaginary part of z)
AINT	**AINT** DINT	R D	R D		AINT (a)	$= \mathrm{INT}\,(a)$ (Typ R or D)
ANINT	**ANINT** **DNINT**	R D	R D	1	ANINT (a)	$= \begin{cases} \mathrm{INT}\,(a + 0.5) & \text{for } a \geqslant 0 \\ \mathrm{INT}\,(a - 0.5) & \text{for } a < 0 \end{cases}$ rounding
NINT	**IDNINT** NINT	I I	D R		NINT (a)	$= \begin{cases} \mathrm{INT}\,(a + 0.5) & \text{for } a \geqslant 0 \\ \mathrm{INT}\,(a - 0.5) & \text{for } a < 0 \end{cases}$
–	**CONJG**	C	C	1	CONJG (z)	$=$ conjg. complex value of z
COS	**CCOS** **DCOS** COS	C D R	C D R	1	COS (a)	$= \cos\,(a)$ a in radian
COSH	COSH **DCOSH**	R D	R D	1	COSH (a)	$= \dfrac{e^a + e^{-a}}{2}$
DIM	**DDIM** DIM IDIM	D R I	D R I	2	DIM (a, b)	$= \begin{cases} a - b & \text{if } a > b \\ 0 & \text{otherwise} \end{cases}$
–	**DPROD**	D	R	2	DPROD (a, b)	$= a \cdot b$ (in double precision)
EXP	**CEXP** **DEXP** EXP	C D R	C D R	1	EXP (a)	$= e^a$
–	**INDEX**	I	ch	2	INDEX (c_1, c_2)	$= \begin{cases} \text{Position in the CHARCTER variable } c_1, \\ \text{begins in the substring } c_2; \\ 0 \text{ if } c_2 \text{ is not included in } c_1 \end{cases}$
	LEN	I	ch	1	LEN (c)	$=$ length of CHARCTER variable c

Bold Type: Only defined in full Fortran 77 and not in the subset.

b) Mathematical Functions (Continuation)

| Name | | Type | | Number of | | |
Generic	Specific	Result	Argument	Arguments	Call	Meaning
LOG	**ALOG** **CLOG** **DLOG**	R C D	R C D	1	LOG (a)	ln (a) (natural logarithm)
LOG10	**ALOG10** **DLOG10**	R D	R D	1	LOG10 (a)	$\log_{10}$ (a)
MAX	**AMAX1** **DMAX** MAX0	R D I	R D I	≥ 2	MAX $(a_1, a_2, ...)$	$= \max (a_1, a_2, ...)$
– –	**AMAX0** MAX1	R I	I R	≥ 2	AMAX0 $(n_1, n_2, ...)$ MAX1 $(x_1, x_2, ...)$	$= \max (n_1, n_2, ...)$ with type $= \max (x_1, x_2, ...)$ transformation
MIN	**AMIN1** **DMIN1** MIN0	R D I	R D I	≥ 2	MIN $(a_1, a_2, ...)$	$= \min (a_1, a_2, ...)$
– –	**AMIN0** MIN1	R I	I R	≥ 2	AMIN0 $(n_1, n_2, ...)$ MIN1 $(x_1, x_2, ...)$	$= \min (n_1, n_2, ...)$ with type $= \min (x_1, x_2, ...)$ transformation
MOD	**AMOD** **DMOD** MOD	R D I	R D I	2	MOD (a, b)	$= a - \mathrm{INT}\left(\dfrac{a}{b}\right) \cdot b$
SIGN	**DSIGN** ISIGN SIGN	D I R	D I R	2	SIGN (a, b)	$= \begin{cases} \|a\| & \text{if } b \geq 0 \\ -\|a\| & \text{if } b < 0 \end{cases}$
SIN	**CSIN** **DSIN** SIN	C D R	C D R	1	SIN (a)	$= \sin (a)$ a in radians
SINH	**DSINH** SINH	D R	D R	1	SINH (a)	$= \dfrac{e^a - e^{-a}}{2}$
SQRT	**CSQRT** **DSQRT** SQRT	C D R	C D R	1	SQRT (a)	$= \sqrt{a}$
TAN	**DTAN** TAN	D R	D R	1	TAN (a)	$= \tan (a)$ a in radians
TANH	**DTANH** TANH	D R	D R	1	TANH (a)	$= \tanh (a)$

c) Comparison Functions for CHARACTER Items

| Name | Type | | Number of | Call | Meaning |
	Result	Argument	Arguments		
LGE	L	ch	2	LGE (c_1, c_2)	lexicographically greater or equal
LGT	L	ch	2	LGT (c_1, c_2)	lexicographically greater
LLE	L	ch	2	LLE (c_1, c_2)	lexicographically smaller or equal
LLT	L	ch	2	LLT (c_1, c_2)	lexicographically smaller

Appendix D: Summary of all Statements

Summary of all Statements as well as Deviations Between Full and Subset Versions of Fortran 77

Executable Statement	Statement	Subset	Page	Meaning
x	ASSIGN m TO v	x	–	Assignment of label m to INTEGER variable v.
x	Assignment statement v = w	x	5, 16	Assignment of a value w to a variable v.
x	BACKSPACE u	x	105	File u is backspaced one record;
x	BACKSPACE (UNIT = u, IOSTAT = v, ERR = s)	–	–	additionally: Status in INTEGER variable v, branching to s for the case of an error.
–	BLOCK DATA	–	94	Initialization of variables in the labeled COMMON area.
x	CALL Name (lap)	x	81	Call of the subroutine Name with the list of actual parameters.
–	CHARACTER *l Variable list	x	61	Declaration of the character variable (length l).
x	CLOSE (UNIT = u, IOSTAT = v, ERR = s, STATUS = z)	–	104	Close of file u, status in INTEGER variable v, branching to s for the case of an error, definition of file status z.
–	COMMON/Name/Variable list	x	90, 93	Definition of COMMON areas.
–	COMPLEX Variable list	–	96	Declaration of complex variables.
x	CONTINUE	x	22	Empty statement (e.g. for the use of labels).
–	DATA Variable list/Constant list/	x	67, 86	Initialization of variables using defined constants; (in subset: no implied DO-loops).
–	DIMENSION Variable list	–	33	Definition of the lower and upper index limits for fields; up to seven dimensions.
		x	33	Definition of upper index limits for fields up to three dimensions.
x	DO n d = a, e, i	–	24	Loop control, d: arithmetic variable; a, e, i: arithmetic expressions.
		x	24	Loop control; d: INTEGER variable; a, e, i: INTEGER constants or variables.
–	DOUBLE PRECISION Variable list	–	15	Declaration of double precision variables.
x	ELSE	x	21	Begin of an alternative block IF statement.
x	ELSE IF (le) THEN	x	23	Comparison of cases for a block IF statement.
x	END	x	6, 73	Final statement of a program segment.
x	END IF	x	21	End of IF block.
x	ENDFILE u	x	104	Writing of the End-of-File label on file u;
x	ENDFILE (UNIT = u, IOSTAT = v, ERR = s)	–	–	additionally: Status in INTEGER variable v, branching to s for the case of an error.
–	ENTRY Name (lfp)	–	–	Definition of an alternative entry of subprogram with respect to its name, type and parameters.
–	EQUIVALENCE (Name list)	x	95	Different names are assigned the same storage place.
–	EXTERNAL Subprogram list	x	77	For external subprograms (as actual parameters).
–	FORMAT (Format-Codes)	x	6, 38	Definition of format for input and output.
–	Type FUNCTION Name (lfp)	x	73	Declaration of a function subprogram; subset: Type CHARACTER not permitted.

Executable Statement	Statement	Subset	Page	Meaning
x	GOTO m	x	16	Skip to label m.
x	GOTO v	x	–	Skip to the label previously assigned to the variable v ($\to$ ASSIGN).
x	GOTO (List of labels) v	x	88	Skip to the ith label, if the variable v has the value i.
x	IF (le) s	x	18	Logical IF.
x	IF (ae) m_1, m_2, m_3	x	21	Arithmetic IF.
x	IF (le) THEN	x	21	Block IF.
–	IMPLICIT Type (Set of letters)	x	33	Implied type definition of (variable) names.
x	INQUIRE (Key word parameter)	–	–	Inquiry about file parameters by means of key words.
–	INTEGER Variable list	x	10	Declaration of integer variables.
–	INTRINSIC Function list	x	78	Characterization of predefined functions.
–	LOGICAL Variable list	x	19	Declaration of Boolean variables.
x	OPEN (Control list)	x	102	Opening of file u; additional parameters control the method of access, record length, file name etc. Subset is subject to limitation.
–	PARAMETER (Name=Const.)	–	32	Definition of names for constant values.
x	PAUSE	x	113	Interrupt (interactive) of output.
x	PRINT f, Output list	–	–	Output on the printer; simplified form of WRITE (*, f) output list.
–	PROGRAM Name	x	–	Definition of the name "Name" for the main program.
x	READ (Control list) Input list	x	52, 103	Reading of data; only a simplified control list allowed in the subset.
x	READ f, Input list	–	–	Reading from the assigned unit; simplified form of READ (*, f) input list.
–	REAL Variable list	x	4	Declaration of real-value variables.
x	RETURN	x	73, 80	Return from subprogram to program segment where the call was made.
x	RETURN n	–	88	In addition for subroutines; Skip to a particular label in the program segment where the call was made.
x	REWIND u	x	105	Positioning to the first record of the file u.
x	REWIND (UNIT = u, IOSTAT = v, ERR = s)	–	–	In addition: Status given to INTEGER variable v, branching to s for the case of an error.
x	SAVE Variable list	x	86	Saving of the variable values in a subprogram call for a call at a later stage.
x	SAVE	–	86	Saving of all variable values in a subprogram call for a call at a later stage.
–	Statement function	x	71	Declaration of a function using a single statement; CHARACTER not allowed in subset.
x	STOP	x	6	Termination of program execution.
–	SUBROUTINE (lfp)	x	80	Declaration of a subroutine; it is not allowed to use * as a formal parameter in the subset.
x	WRITE (Control list) Output list	x	6, 38	Transfer of data to a file; in subset: Only a simplified control list.

Appendix E: ASCII Character Code

The unit for storing characters consists of 7 bits and it can thought of as being arranged in the following manner:

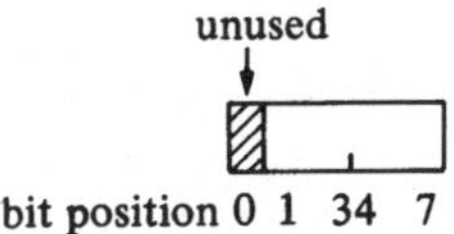

The first two lines of the following table as well as the last position contain the coding of the control information for the operating system.

position 4–7	0	1	2	3	4	5	6	7	8	9	A	B	C	D	E	F
Bit-position 1–3 0	NUL	SOH	STX	ETX	EOT	ENQ	ACK	BEL	BS	HT	LF	VT	FF	CR	SO	SI
1	DLE	DC1	DC1	DC3	DC4	NAK	SYN	ETB	CAN	EM	SUB	ESC	FS	GS	RS	US
2		!	"	#	$	%	&	'	(	)	*	+	,	–	.	/
3	0	1	2	3	4	5	6	7	8	9	:	;	<	=	>	?
4	@	A	B	C	D	E	F	G	H	I	J	K	L	M	N	O
5	P	Q	R	S	T	U	V	W	X	Y	Z	[	\	]	^	_
6	`	a	b	c	d	e	f	g	h	i	j	k	l	m	n	o
7	p	q	r	s	t	u	v	w	x	y	z	{	|	}	~	DEL

Meaning of the abbreviations

ACK	Acknowledge		FS	File Separator
BEL	Bell		GS	Group Separator
BS	Backspace		HT	Horizontal Tabulation
CAN	Cancel		LF	Line Feed
CR	Carriage Return		NAK	Negative Acknowledge
DC	Device Control Characters		NUL	Null
DEL	Delete		RS	Record Separator
DLE	Data Link Escape		SI	Shift-in
EM	End of Medium		SO	Shift-out
ENQ	Enquiry		SOH	Start of Heading
EOT	End of Transmission		STX	Start of Text
ESC	Escape		SUB	Substitute Character
ETB	End of Transmission Block		SYN	Synchronous Idle
ETX	End of Text		US	Unit Separator
FF	Format Feed		VT	Vertical Tabulation

Index